The Beauty Behind My Darkness

A collection of poems

By

Michael Tavon

The Beauty Behind My Darkness
by
Michael Tavon

After you finish reading, please leave a review on Amazon or Goodreads. Word of mouth is the biggest vehicle for pushing a book, so, please leave a review, post your favorite pieces on social media, or tell a friend! Any gesture goes a long way. Thank you.

The Beauty Behind my Darkness
by
Michael Tavon

Other Works

Poetry Collections

Nirvana: Pieces of Self-Healing vol 1
Nirvana: Pieces of Self-Healing vol.2
Songs for Each Mood
Songs For Each Mood Vol.2
Don't Wait Til I Die to Love Me
Don't Wait Til I Die to Love Me vol. II
Don't Wait Til I Die to Love Me Vol. III
Young Heart, Old Souls
The Pisces
Dreaming in a Perfect World
To Build a Home
A Home for Lonely Souls

Fictitious Novels

God is a Woman
Far from Heaven

Other Works

Heal, Inspire, Love w/ Moonsouldchild
Self-Talks w/ Moonsoulchild

Spoken Word Albums

The Beauty Behind My Darkness
Dreaming in a Perfect World
Nirvana: Pieces of Self-Healing
To Build a Home
Don't Wait til I Die to Love Me 1 & 2

The Beauty Behind My Darkness
by
Michael Tavon

Amazon Self-Publishing
Kindle Direct Publishing

© 2023 by Michael Tavon
All rights reserved, including the rights to reproduce this book or portions thereof in any form whatsoever.

All contents are original works by author, Michael Tavon, any redistribution without the author's consent is illegal.

Posting any content from this book without crediting the author is considered plagiarism.

The Beauty Behind my Darkness
by
Michael Tavon

Important Message from the Author

This poetry collection is a true labor of love. Many of you may not relate to the pieces of each section, but I hope you can look outside of your personal experiences and see the work for what it is... art. I don't know why, but poetry has become a medium for most readers to relate to or assist in their personal development. I'll be the first to say I am always deeply flattered when someone says my work is relatable in some way, but that is not the main goal when publishing my work. Sometimes poetry is fun and lighthearted

I want to share my growth, my story, and my talent with the world, and if it helps people along the way, it is a wonderful connection to share. Remember, if my work isn't relatable to you, it doesn't mean it is not worthy of respect or can't be enjoyed. Most of us listen to songs, watch films, and read novels we don't relate to, but we still love them because they make us feel something. And suppose you exclusively consume any form of art for its relatability. In that case, you are missing out on an entire world of incredible art. So, I just ask you to read my work with a full heart and open mind. I promise you'll enjoy and respect my labor in each piece. Even if you conclude that my work isn't for you, I hope you can still feel the passion and love behind my work.

To wrap this message up, I divided this collection into four sections to make your reading experience as smooth as possible.

Section I explores the themes of failed relationships, dating during this modern (social media) era, and the mixed emotions that come with them such as jealousy, confusion, ego, and fear. It took a lot to put my flaws and mistakes on full display. These poems tell a story of my mindset during my early twenties. I was not always the hero, nor was I always the victim. I've never been the type of male poet to pretend I was a knight in shining armor to sell more books; that's not me. I am a lover who has made poor choices. I write about them so readers can see any possible red flags in future dating prospects or even use these poems to help prevent them from making the same mistakes I made.

Section II is about the road to self-discovery we embark on after heartbreak and after realizing it's time to heal from the trauma we endured throughout our lives. This isn't all flowers and butterflies. Sometimes times, healing can get dark and messy, too. To grow into the best version of yourself, you have to dig deep and do the inner work.

Section III is all about the healthy love we discover after going through the ups and downs of life. This section is my most personal and experimental. I share intimate details of the love I have found with Moonsoulchild from the time we met to before our wedding day. I've also experimented with different forms of poems like Sonku and Tanka. Which was really fun. I hope my story and perspective can inspire millions of hopeful romantics to never give up on finding their person because they are out there.

So read the sections in the order you prefer and tell me your favorite section(s) via social media. Much love. Thank you.

The Beauty Behind my Darkness
by
Michael Tavon

The Beauty Behind
My Darkness

The Beauty Behind My Darkness
by
Michael Tavon

Illustration Credits

I'd like to give a special thanks to Alexandra Craig for designing the book cover, you can follow her at

Twitter: @craig_AlexG
IG: ArtVia Alex

I also have to thank my brother Woodrow Butler for the other illustrations
IG: @officialwoesk

The rest of the illustrations were found on the Canva app.

The Beauty Behind my Darkness
by
Michael Tavon

Section I

Where the Sun Doesn't Shine

The Beauty Behind My Darkness
by
Michael Tavon

The Beauty Behind my Darkness
by
Michael Tavon

I Thought it Was Real

I used to dream of the day you would
Love me the way I loved you.

I would hope for the day
The connection became infectious,
And energies would finally sync
To flow on the same wavelength.
Despite exhausting my efforts,
The chemistry lacked
A key element to thrive.

You refused to love me the way
I loved you and I wish I knew why
All the warning signs
Flashed like flare guns.
But I was convinced
We were primed
For something special.

I would let my imagination run
Wild like a child on a playground.
I knew one day,
You'd come to your senses;
I had all the time in the world for you
And I was willing to wait.

I saw a future between us;
You saw a dead end before
Our journey began
When I snapped back into reality.
I was a pathetic mess.
With lost time I would never get back

The Beauty Behind My Darkness
by
Michael Tavon

Funerals & You

I shouldn't have
To bury the unique
Parts of myself
To keep a relationship alive.

If you're too insecure
It will be impossible for me to thrive.
I must save myself before I transform
Into someone I can't recognize.

My heart is a garden,
Not a funeral home
If you don't support my growth,
I won't let you spit venom
Into the soil of my soul.

The Beauty Behind my Darkness
by
Michael Tavon

Cutting Ties

Our tryst has reached the end of its trial.
No more lies, we've lost
All reason to smile; it's best to cut ties
While we still adore the good times.

No tug-of-war;
Let me go; we must end.
An easy heartbreak
Makes for a softer mend.

We can't be friends;
We'll fade into strangers,
Once again.

It wasn't you; it wasn't me.
It was fate, we're not meant to be.

You will find a grander love;
I won't hold you back.
My pretty bird, I set you free.

Fly…fly…rise high,
Leave me behind.
I'm sorry, this is the end
Of our line.

Fly far away.
See what life brings.
My pretty bird, use those pretty wings.

The Beauty Behind My Darkness
by
Michael Tavon

Apologies from a Deadbeat Lover

I'm sorry I hurt you in more ways.
Ten fingers can count.
I'm sorry, our love went south.
It's my fault, we got lost
And you had to reroute
To make it out.

I'm sorry for the emotional wars.
My sweetie,
Let's sign us a peace treaty.
Please forgive me.
I know it was hard to love me,
But I'll make leaving me easy.

I was a deadbeat lover,
More childish than Donald Glover.
You will find another person
Who will treat you like royalty,
In the streets and under the covers.

I've said sorry,
Till the meaning wore off.
I created the wound
And tore the bandage off.

Take my baggage off your shoulders
So you can have
The strength to leave.
It's finally over.
You've been high off my lies;
It's time to go sober.
This is your closure.

I'll leave you be; this is the final part.
No more empty promises,
I'll quit breaking your heart.

The Wanderer

The thought of fading from
This life crossed my mind
At least a dozen times,
In a crowded darkness
of heavy cries.

I never understood why,
I couldn't fathom why.

Why did I want to die?
I needed to solve this problem
But depression doesn't
Need a reason to prosper.

Depression is a wanderer,
Searching for a new home
And will settle in any heart
That feels alone.

And that's where I was
A few inches above rock bottom.
Depression said, *Got him.*
It felt hot as hell in autumn.

I was ready to end my fate
Till a voice in my head said,
Heaven Can Wait
Please stop, heaven can wait.
It wasn't my time to escape,
It was time to make a change.

The Beauty Behind My Darkness
by
Michael Tavon

Waterfalls and Rivers

My resilient heart
Refused to succumb to the agony.
I transformed my river of tears
Into a waterfall of hope.

No troubled waters
Formed against me shall drown
This ravishing soul of mine.

The Beauty Behind my Darkness
by
Michael Tavon

My Farewell Too

Some days I feel like I'm chasing a dream
That has no desire to become a reality.

It seems like I'm planting seeds
In concrete where there's no hope for my garden to grow.

Grey hairs sprout from my scalp
When I stress over the factors I can't control.

Am I doing anything right?
What am I doing wrong?

These thoughts loom over like a dark cloud
With no silver lining.
I try to find a light
That doesn't want to find me.

The universe often sends signs
To provide some temporary happiness,
But I desire the everlasting.

To save my mental health,
I've decided to take a step back,
And for the best.

I've put in the work ten times over.
If destiny is meant to be,
The good things will come to me.

The Beauty Behind My Darkness
by
Michael Tavon

10.22.2016

I'm living off a prayer,
I hope it comes true.
I've been dreaming of colors:
 Most of them are blue
Dwelling in the grey.
I hope summer remains the same,
A picture of peace
Behind these rose-tinted frames,
Darkness along the horizon,
Yet I stand alone in silence
Smiling amid the storm's violence
Because the ugly won't hurt.
I promise.

I promise,
Even though I'm lost,
I refuse to be gone.
I won't die alone.
This heart will remain gold.
It won't turn to stone.

The Beauty Behind my Darkness
by
Michael Tavon

10.16.2015

We all are going to die.
It's set in stone.
We all smile when it shines
And cry when it's gone
All alone in this hell hole.
On earth do we belong?
Only heaven knows.

Happiness is a rental,
Because you are going to return it
Why is pain so natural?
But love we have to earn it.
We are concerned with
Bridges not burning
And tables not turning.
Life is the lesson we learn.
On the fly,
 There are no guides or handbooks
On how to stay alive.
It's ironic because it's a million ways to die.
 There are thousand gods in the sky
But when I ask for strength,
They barely reply.

For Sale

My heart is not up for sale
Nor is it up for rent.
I'm not looking for a temporary tenant,
I'm ready for someone
Who desires to spend
The rest of their days in this temple
When they finally enter.

The Beauty Behind my Darkness
by
Michael Tavon

You Don't Have to Say it

You need to know how I feel
Even if you don't feel the same.
I know you're too afraid
To let down your guard
Because being vulnerable
Seems like a death trap.

I love you,
Even if you don't say it back,
How I feel about you
Won't break over the words
You don't say.

The Beauty Behind My Darkness
by
Michael Tavon

The Crush/The Rejection

I'm too tongue-tied
To express how
Deeply I want you.
There's an anxious fight between
The heart and mind.
I want you to be mine,
But the fear of rejection
Paralyzes my confidence.
The awkwardness
Takes over my body.
Sweet nothings become stale,
In the heat of nervous despair.
I stutter over my words
Like my thoughts were written
In doctor's cursive.
My curse is being stuck
In my own head.
I want you,
But my heart thinks.
Those feelings are better
Left unsaid.

The Beauty Behind my Darkness
by
Michael Tavon

Sparing Partner With Disappointment

I'm so immune to disappointment,
I barely feel the burn when it stings
Like a wasp with a vendetta.

Am I hopeful or just hope's fool
As I keep tugging on love's rope
With the notion my efforts
won't go in vain.

I keep putting my best foot forward
But I stumble over every crack
on the pavement; as i chase the idea
Of someone wanting me back

Such a sad life to lead,
A heart that bleeds honesty
In a world that avoids reciprocity,

What's wrong with me?
Why am I cursed with loneliness?

Sometimes the hardest heartbreak is losing
The love you never had,
Losing the love you imagined inside
Your idealistic head

I saw her, and myself
Lying in bed, for years to come
I envisioned children,
The beautiful home, and growing together
Then that dream got crushed

By the powerful blows of rejection,
The opponent I can't fight back .

The Beauty Behind My Darkness
by
Michael Tavon

All I can do is lean against the ropes
And take the blows one by one
Until my body goes numb

I'm done with love,
Since disappointment is all I've ever known
I've lost all hope,
My optimism is dead and gone

Still Night, Silent Cry

The suffering grows
When left alone

A cry for help goes unheard
When the night is still,
Illusions confuse the mind
Between what's real and what to feel
A body filled with cold chills

The suffering grows
When left alone

Loneliness is a parasite
That kills the gardens
In your soul,
Without self-love
Nothing grows

But the suffering
when left alone

Snooze

I close my eyes
To recall an echo
Of a past time.
The voice sings of yesteryear
I yearn to hear,
Waking me up
To remind me of
The time I felt most alive
Before the moment
Slips through the crevices
Of my mind.

Closed for Business: Emotionally Unavailable

It was a weird space to have full access
To your body with restrictions to your mind.
I thought you had something to hide.
You allowed my hands to sensually surf
Along the waves of your skin,
But deep dives into your heart were forbidden.

Asking for permission turned
Into begging for forgiveness.
When you said your heart was not open for business,
I should've listened,
But I kept insisting,
Hoping you would reconsider.
Let me enter the parts you were reluctant to bear,
To you, this was just a physical affair.

An attraction this fatal left our connection unstable.
When I put my trust on the table
You said you were emotionally unavailable.
Confusion clouded my mind.
How could someone give all of their loving,
But only half the time reeling me close enough
While remaining distant at the same time?

In the end, I only had myself to blame.
Emotionally unavailable is not a game to be played.
When it comes to love I shouldn't have to convince
Anyone's heart to change.

The Beauty Behind My Darkness
by
Michael Tavon

I will not chase a love
That runs in circles.
I will not beg for affection
or compete for attention.
May the love I deserve
Attract to me like magnets
After revealing
My feelings
To you.

The Beauty Behind my Darkness
by
Michael Tavon

Talk it Out

We've come too far to let this clash
Break us apart.
Instead of casting stones,
Let's speak from the heart.

Let's find a common ground and sit down,
Till we talk it out; no *he said, she said,*
Eliminate any room for doubt.

Your point of view is as valid as mine.
Let's take the time to recognize each other's minds.
There's no need to yell, fight, or cry.

We're mature enough to find a solution
Without causing more pain.
In this new edition of our love,
Can you stand the rain?

No more bars and chains let's be free.
Before we go to sleep can we please,
Release this negative energy between you and me?

Sleep on it

You are starving for an argument
But I don't speak in fallacies.
Our stars do not align.
Actually, we live in different galaxies

See, love is in an art piece
But I don't wanna be
Another casualty
In your gallery.

Because I'm not fond of wasting time,
Tell me what's on your mind.

Please don't leave this issue
Hanging on by a thread-
Passive aggressive threads
Left on read.
We're too grown to leave
The truth unsaid.
We could either sleep on it
Or clear this out,
Before we go to bed.

The Beauty Behind my Darkness
by
Michael Tavon

Messy Social Media Breakup

Stressing over you
Was like pouring tears into a flood,
Little impact was made.
Too much damage had been done.
I fought to keep my hands clean
While you dragged my name
Through the mud.
I gave the best version of myself
 But it was never enough.
You concealed the truth
By making it all up
Departing from us
Wasn't even the worst;
It was the false narrative
You shared with the world
Instead of keeping your mouth shut.
We could've split amicably,
But you caused a storm
Through a one-sided-subliminal war.
I dodged the friendly fire
And escaped unscathed
Amidst the disappointment.
I discovered a better moment.
I saw your true colors.
You were desperate for attention
And chased the drama to feel
Superior.

The Beauty Behind My Darkness
by
Michael Tavon

A Pathetic Kind of Feeling

I used to dream of you
Loving me the way you love him.

Where was all that P.D.A
When I was with you?
You never held my hand
The way you clutch his.
Were you ashamed of me?

You never celebrated my dreams
The way you crown him king.
I'm not jealous;
I just need to know why.
Didn't you believe in me?

Your smile has a different curve.
Your skin has a glow and compliments
Your texture.

Did you hold your true self
Captive until you found someone else?

I can tell by the way you stare
At him, you see everything
You couldn't see in me.
I guess you were farsighted
When it came to noticing the real me.

Where did you learn to love?
Who taught you?
Your persona could've fooled me.
The way you loved me,
I thought your heart lacked the capacity.

The Beauty Behind my Darkness
by
Michael Tavon

Maybe I wasn't that influential.
My presence wasn't sublime.
Maybe he was the one you
Wanted to be with the whole damn time.

I should've listened to my intuition
When it warned me about you,
When you said he wasn't someone
To worry about.
Deep down, I knew it wasn't true.

A Feeling I Don't Like

Why am I suddenly jealous over you?
You're free to do what you want to do.

Am I selfish for wanting you for myself?
You're no possession, but you belong
To no one else.

I get 38 hot when
You mention another name
Burning a fever of envy
Over my flame.

How could another have your attention?
Am I not enough?
Is there something missing
Between us?

This awkward phase of
Knowing what I want
But fighting what I feel,
Are they just a placeholder
Or is it something real?

Maybe you're waiting for me
To stop sleeping on you.
I hope I wake up before
It's too late.
This feeling is too raw, scary, and new.

The Beauty Behind my Darkness
by
Michael Tavon

Far from Home

Heartache is a destination far from home.
We lost ourselves and you were left
To find your way back all alone.

You were alone all along
Trying to fit your heart
Into a space that didn't belong.

From the start, we didn't belong.
We just prolonged the imminent
Guilt trips for the innocent.

The innocent lover suffered
The harshest sentence,
While the criminal is viewed from a distance.

I created distance by staying close to you,
A magic trick only a few can master.
Lies turn love into a natural disaster.

I was a natural disaster
That turned diamonds into stones.
Heartbreak is a destination far from home.

The Beauty Behind My Darkness
by
Michael Tavon

I've trusted too many
times before.
Look where it has gotten
me,
Deserted with days of
self-loathing.

If I open my half-
empty heart again
While it's on the mend,
Would you replenish it,
Or take what I have left
And finish it?

Let me know before it's too late

The Beauty Behind my Darkness
by
Michael Tavon

When Potential Becomes an Illusion

Your patience gets tested
As you wait for them
To become who they
Pretend to be.
They dilute the truth
With watered-down promises.

As a master of disguise,
They buy enough time
To keep you around
With the illusion
Of potential.
They know how to
Kindly confuse you.

You see the world in them,
But the connection
Is rooted in a lie.

Before becoming a pawn in their chess game,
Take off those rose-tinted frames
To see the true hues
Behind their fake smiles.

Waiting for them to realize
Their *potential,*
Is like waiting for a plane
At a train station.
You'll be stuck with hours wasted
And no closer to your destination.

The Beauty Behind My Darkness
by
Michael Tavon

Promiscuous Pessimist

Sharing this bed with body after body,
 And hoping something lasting comes from it
Has left me feeling less than nothing.

Soul-crushing intimacy, arid stares
In the dark, yearning for closeness,
With our minds miles apart,
We kiss with no spark,
Skin to skin, with detaching hearts,

Sex feels like a cold wind
On nude skin.
We bare ourselves until
An empty climax, a connection
With unlatched affection.
We starve for something real.
Our bodies reveal the truth
Our hearts refuse to feel.

This bed has seen so many bodies,
Carried a lot of weight.
If my mattress could talk,
What would it say? Would it be ashamed?

I am trying to find a spouse
In a stranger at 2 am.
Who I am? This lifestyle is so dumb.
My heart is tired, my pride is numb.
A promiscuous pessimist-
That is what I've become.

The Beauty Behind My Darkness
by
Michael Tavon

Big Love in a Shallow Pond

My heart was never too ***deep;***
Your capacity to comprehend
My passions
Were too
Shallow.

I'm not at fault
For having a
Heart of gold.
You're at fault
For making me
Feel wrong for
Providing the
strongest love,
When you could've left me alone.

The Beauty Behind My Darkness
by
Michael Tavon

Closure Again

You don't deserve
To take another chapter
From my life.
There's no need to finish,
Let's skip the climax.
I already know
How this story
Is going to end.

The Beauty Behind My Darkness
by
Michael Tavon

If they call you insecure
After crossing a boundary
You've established many times,
It's not honesty,
It's a form of emotional abuse.

The Beauty Behind My Darkness
by
Michael Tavon

A Headache Called Dating

Baby, I could be your future,
Or I could be your past.
The fate is determined by
How you treat me and how you act.
I graduated from the games;
You're still in the back of the class.
Try me again, that will be your last.
I love hard but I'll bolt Usain, fast.

But if you want real love, you can have it.
I'm strong enough to carry
Your emotional baggage.

As long as you don't do me dirt
And leave me embarrassed,
I prefer to stay low like a stratus
But if you wanna chase clout, keep running
Till you feel off-balanced.

I'm not a side dish, baby.
I'm a full meal.
Who's ol' dude in your comments
Keep it more than real?
I am not afraid to reveal my heart
And show you how I feel,
But telling the truth
Seems to be your Achilles heel.
If you have trust issues,
Take some time to heal.
I don't wanna get dizzy
Playing the run-around.
How could I lift you up
If you refuse to hold me down?
My intentions are clear.
Do you want me to stick around?

The Beauty Behind My Darkness
by
Michael Tavon

Verse 2

If I give you all my love
I want more than half of your time.
You're running up my mileage
With the gas light.
You're acting like you weren't with
Some other dude last night.
It's cool, you have options.
So, don't be fake modest.
I'd respect you more
For being honest.
But why do you trip
When you see me in other girl's comments?
This ill affair is starting to sound toxic.
I got it, you want me to yourself
While belonging to the streets.
You keep playing this song on repeat,
Crying about trust,
When it's you that are with the tricks and deceit.
Either you're all in or step out.
My love is an ocean;
There will never be a drought.

The Beauty Behind My Darkness
by
Michael Tavon

This is My Time

If you don't have the foresight
To believe in my dreams,
When you see me
Putting in the work,
Leave expeditiously.
I have no desire to share
My sacred space with people
Who have clouds of doubt
Raining over them.
I don't need another
Storm in my life.
Even a broken clock can see
When my time is coming.
Why can't you?

The Beauty Behind My Darkness
by
Michael Tavon

Heartache and Residuals

I understand that your ex
Was a waste of mental space,
And you're left empty like
A finished Thanksgiving plate.
All they did was take, take, and take
While you gave all your love and time.
Their vibe was far from sublime.
You felt hogtied by their tricks and lies.
All the while, their pretty smile was
The weapon they used to disarm you,
Till broken promises felt like the truth.
Now, everything I say or do you second guess
Like multiple choice on a math test
This added stress, puts a strain on us,
Making me tread on a tightrope of faith.
Slow down, there's no need to rush.
I am not the one who hurt you.
Why let your unhealed past fuck us up?
No ultimatum, But here is my truth:
I refuse to suffer From secondhand trust issues.
I am not your ex, I am not about to go broke
Paying for their mistakes.
Please spare me the residual heartbreak.

The Beauty Behind My Darkness
by
Michael Tavon

Another Poem about Anxiety, I Fear

Anxiety has the forethought
To warn me about memories lost
In hindsight.

It's a wizard who can see
The storms of tomorrow,
But unsighted to the sunset
Along the horizon.

A constraint, a complaint
As it echoes the forbidden things
I dare not say when I wish to move ahead.

Never a positive reinforcement
Nor a motivating factor;
Its laughter bellows in my tight belly.

There's no stopping its arrival;
My undefeated rival I fight
Till I find a way to win.

The Beauty Behind My Darkness
by
Michael Tavon

The Nervous System

It first starts in the mind
When thoughts become a dark hole,
Without a rope to climb,
You're stuck and all alone.

Then your heart loses its cool.
Like a quiet kid who gets bullied
In school, you cry for help
But can't be heard over
The boisterous crowd
You've constructed in your head.

This feeling attacks
Every inch of your body,
Until a weak spot is spotted,
Then antagonizes you
By taunting your inability
To fight it off.

Anxiety is the oppressor
Keeping you from a calm life,
But never forget you're more than
Strong enough to push back.

The Beauty Behind My Darkness
by
Michael Tavon

The Potential

Your 'potential'
Was just a figment
In my imagination,
Based on the dreams you sold.
As I slept on the truth,
I woke up habitually
Disappointed by you.
You never aspired to be better.
I can only blame myself
For being entrapped
By the potential
You never had the intention
To live up to.

The Beauty Behind My Darkness
by
Michael Tavon

Her Last Relationship

She was stuck in a love
Of very little motion
With the notion, it would
Go back to what it used to be.

Day after day,
She became content
In a sluggish love.
Finding comfort in a bond
That was falling apart.

Happiness slowly wafted away
As the person she sleeps with
Began to feel like a stranger.
Filled with silent anger,
She managed to keep
A smile on her face.

With less quality time
And empty affection,
Lack of gravity pulled them
In opposite directions.

Her intuition said it was time
To leave everything behind.
She was strong enough to say goodbye.
She was brave enough to create a better life.

The Beauty Behind My Darkness
by
Michael Tavon

Despite our flame
Being rained on,
How I feel about you
Will never subside.
I still care, and will always
Wish the best for you.

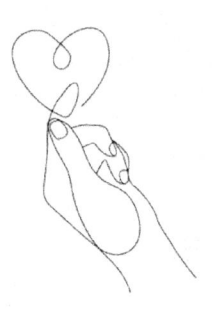

The Beauty Behind My Darkness
by
Michael Tavon

Why Were You Going Through my Phone?

Did I give you a reason to not trust me?
Are we too good to be true that
You had to dig for a disappointment?
Was it worth it?

Tears escape your eyes
Over text replies from years prior,
Trying to make me out to be a liar
Over words I never said
 And searching for secrets that don't exist.

I understand you're more cautious
After trusting the wrong ones.
I'm not them, do you feel me?

This is passion in rare form.
There's no need to go
Through my phone.
Whatever you need to know,
I'll give it to you raw,
No sugar coat.

I need you to believe
In the words, I speak.
Doubt shall not seep
Into your mind,
When you gaze at me.

The Beauty Behind My Darkness
by
Michael Tavon

Facts Tho

You were right,
I didn't love you.
I loved the idea of you.
I never took the time
To gradually fall for you.
I wasn't a student of your heart.
I failed the course.

Pushing my affection
Was a weight you didn't deserve
To carry.

For that, I apologize.

I was a lonely soul
With picket fence dreams.
When I saw you, I imagined
Two kids, a house, and a ring.

My mind skipped the journey
And landed at the destination.
Love takes more effort than imagination.

I fell for the idea of being in love
Instead of being with you.

It's all my fault,
I take all accountability
For the time lost
And the heartache I caused you.
I not only hurt you,
I destroyed myself too.

The Beauty Behind My Darkness
by
Michael Tavon

Something Unrequited

I will reserve a piece of my
Heart for you
When you grow tired of running
Through my mind.
You will always have
A place to rest and call home.

The Beauty Behind My Darkness
by
Michael Tavon

Vivid Heartbreak

The pain remains vivid.
Shades of your emotional misuse
Has turned me into a shadow
Of who I used to be.
The biggest heartache
Wasn't losing you;
It was a disappointment
Of breaking the promise
I made to myself
When I vowed to never
Go all out for anyone
Who would refuse
To meet me halfway.

The Beauty Behind My Darkness
by
Michael Tavon

Regrets From Your Ex

I hope they treat you
The way I never did
While I had your heart.
You deserve it.
I got too comfortable,
Taking your affection for granted.
When your lips needed to speak,
I muted your thoughts.
When your tears rained,
I didn't provide sunshine
After the storm.
My pain became yours,
Then I pushed you away
As crippling as it is to say.
You deserve better,
You got it and I'm genuinely
Happy for you.
So, farewell.
I'll be better next lifetime.

The Beauty Behind My Darkness
by
Michael Tavon

The Aftermath of Heartache

Heartbreak has morphed your soul into a cold and lonely stone because you refuse to travel down the road of hope again.

You'd rather remain closed off because you believe Opening up is a risk not worth taking.

To feel safe, you push away any chance of happiness. but how long do you think this facade will sustain?

You're allowed to grieve over the time
That was erased off your clock.

You can cry over the lies you believed when disarmed and naive. You're stronger than you were before.

After you find the tranquility in being alone, trust your heart enough to be soft again.

The Beauty Behind My Darkness
by
Michael Tavon

Colorblind

Turning red flags into green lights,
My eyes were color blind.
When it came to you,
I refused to accept the signs.

After fixing my vision,
A switch flickered in my heart.
I couldn't be mad at you.
You were a piece of shit from the start.

It was my fault for expecting
An Angry bee to not sting.
My lonely heart made me
Tolerate hellish things.

I saw your true hues before it was too late,
In the wake of this heartache,
You will always be remembered
As a mistake, I didn't have to make.

The Beauty Behind My Darkness
by
Michael Tavon

A Disease That Kills

This menace
Is a force of nature
That is too beastly
To tame.

When torn between
Good and wrong,
Selfless and selfish,
Apathy and apologies;
Empathy rots like bad fruit,
Foresight grows dark
And intuition cracks
like glass under heat.

Ego gets in the way
If not taking any blame.
This compulsion
To go against the grain,
Will push everything
That matters away
Until loneliness
Becomes a home.

Pride is a disease
That will kill
Your chance of
A happy ending.

The Beauty Behind My Darkness
by
Michael Tavon

Spades

Dealing with the pain
Like a deck of cards;
Heart on the table,
Shuffling emotions
With unstable hands
Grief is in demand
And the stakes are high
Diggin' this plot
With three spades,
Far from saved.
Taking the wrong chances
Might make this home
a grave.

The Beauty Behind My Darkness
by
Michael Tavon

A Message From a friend After a Breakup

Stop pouring tears over them.
They never cared enough to spare your feelings.
Their lips said sorry,
But their actions expressed otherwise.
They didn't give enough fucks
To hide or cover their tracks.
They knew you'd be weak enough
To take them back.
This might sound like an attack,
But I'm keeping it real.
The hurt they carved into
Your heart was intentional.
They cut so deeply into your flesh
The scars will make sure
You'll never forget their presence
Their unpleasant essence became embedded
Into the waves of your brain,
You'll never feel the same
So, fuck 'em.
Don't drive yourself insane
Wasting prayers that will never get answered
As long as the power is in their hands,
Change will never come.
Wash your palms clean of their dirt
Your heart is too big
to be this hurt .
My friend, you're better off alone.

The Beauty Behind My Darkness
by
Michael Tavon

Section II

Chasing Sunsets:

(The Self-Love Process)

The Beauty Behind My Darkness
by
Michael Tavon

Failure: Rebranded

I've failed more times than I've succeeded
But that never stop me from breathing;
Never stopped me from needing a reason
To keep my heart pumping and beating.
They say gluttony is a sin,
Well smite me for being greedy
I have an appetite for proving
my inner doubts wrong.
That's why I turn my fears into poems
My heartaches into a song
Like Dwayne Johnson, I am Rock strong
And stead. I am ready to conquer
Everything that moves me.
I might turn life into a lifetime movie,
Or Tyler Perry…if the money is right.
I've done more wrong than right
While trying to do what's right,
The irony.
So many wrinkles in my past
This heart on my sleeve
Needed some ironing.
I've failed more times than I've succeeded
But the never stop me from loving,
never stop me from crying,
I was like D.M.X, slipping
But giving up was harder than trying
Wise words from Yeezy,
Believe me when I say
I wasn't born yesterday,
Or the day after,
Ink splattered emotions
Kept me focus,
I got heartbroken three times in
One year— a hat trick

The Beauty Behind My Darkness
by
Michael Tavon

I stretched across my mattress
But never slept on my dreams.
My self-esteem was the steam I needed
To empower me.

But I've failed more times than I've succeeded
And I am still here, still standing I'm still strong.
And I'll keep trying until the breath in my lungs is gone. I'll keep singing until last song has been sung.
There's no quit in my bones,
My heart is only filled with love.

I will continue to fall and get up,
Whether it's with help or by myself
Because to try
Is a success within itself.
I love myself too much to quit
I believe in myself enough
To prevail, I turn dust into gold
My presence will blaze a trail

The Beauty Behind My Darkness
by
Michael Tavon

The Key to Feeling Good

A small act of kindness,
Has the power to unlock
The joy inside a heart
That's chained by anguish,

Don't hesitate to say something nice
When it crosses your mind,
A sweet compliment could last a mile
When it travels to the ears of those
Who need hear your pleasant words the most

Compassion has a lasting effect
When you have enough to spare
Today is the perfect day to show
How much you care

Make this world a brighter place;
Every smile is a poem
Composed of meaningful words

The art of kindness is a gift that gives
Everyone the chance to create
Something wondrous

The Beauty Behind My Darkness
by
Michael Tavon

A Message to My Inner Child

Thank you for being hardheaded
When the world shamed you for
Thinking outside of the box
They tried to detain you in.
Now I'm a free spirit
That's too elusive
To roam in a comfort zone.
Thank you for not growing up too soon;
You took all the time needed.
You never fretted a late bloom.

Now I compete against no one.
I thrive in my own time.
Thank you for having
A thirst for knowledge.
You always asked questions
Until your mind
Got the seeds it needed to grow.
I'm never lost when my intuition
Leads the path because my heart always
 Knows the right way to go.

Despite getting battered during
Your battle to adulthood,
You were strong enough to not allow
This hell we've called home for so long
Strip you of your identity.
You've always been special,
You've always been gold,
I'm so proud of you
Without you, I have
No clue what I would do.

The Beauty Behind My Darkness
by
Michael Tavon

Spades

Dealing with the pain
Like a deck of cards;
heart on the table,
Shuffling emotions
With unstable hands
Grief is in demand
And the stakes are high
Diggin' this plot
With three spades,
Far from saved
Taking the wrong chances
Might make this home
a grave

Selfless

With a heart so selfless,
you never hesitate to lend
A hand to elevate the people around you.
While holding the world's weight in your palms,

You lose stability trying to balance
and keep it all together.
There's no harm in supporting others,
but always prioritize yourself

When it's time to revitalize your spirit.
You can't help your loved ones
if there's nothing left of yourself to give.

The Beauty Behind My Darkness
by
Michael Tavon

Tomorrow isn't Promised, Why Obsess Over it

You're always chasing after mountains and waterfalls.
You never take the time to appreciate
The little hills or creeks in front of you.
You're always running towards
your next big move-
Your next love,
Your next job,
Your next decision,
 And your next adventure.
You wonder why you're tired all day
and restless at night?
Chasing tomorrow has led you
to the dead end of yesterday.
When was the last time
you took a deep breath
And appreciated the air you have today?
Are you so afraid of the moment
that you hide behind the goals you've created
for a future that doesn't exist?
Slow down, and celebrate the life you have now
Before you turn grey with wrinkles of regret;
Pondering over the years of youth
you spent chasing after what's next.

The Beauty Behind My Darkness
by
Michael Tavon

The Beauty in Getting Older

I see things clearer.
I see things for what they are.
I see things for what they could be.
I enjoy moving slowly to enjoy
every vivid detail of my surroundings.
I prefer less crowded spaces,
mom and pop joints,
And undiscovered local gems,
The places people overlook
in lieu of the high life.
Too much noise gives me migraines.
Solitude is my best friend.
I've developed the habit of saying,
"I love you" when closing a conversation.
I look forward to long nature walks.
Afternoon naps rejuvenate me.
I smile more often
 because life makes more sense.
The beauty of getting older is realizing
Most things I stressed about never mattered.
Getting older is the process of letting go
of the dead weight holding you back
And becoming a lighter
Version of who you used to be.

The Beauty Behind My Darkness
by
Michael Tavon

This is Your Fucking Life Yo

You're living on borrowed time
But every minute is yours to own.
Don't waste precious moments
Living for the people who don't walk
In your shoes.
Some would complain
About the fit being too snug;
Others would say the sole is too wide.

Why waste an ounce of life chasing
A life that doesn't suit you?
You were not
Birthed onto this earth to do
What anyone expects you to do.
You are not a vessel for others
To live vicariously through.

Have a dozen children.
Have none at all.
Pursue the career of your dreams.
Even if that dream
Seems far removed from reality,
Feel free to work
The same 9-5 for twenty years
as long as you're content.
Make silly content on social media
If it makes you feel confident.

Settle down with the love of your life
Or screw as many people as you want.
Live as a free spirit or follow a religion.
Whatever makes you smile chase that
Until you die.

Be a party animal or be a homebody.

The Beauty Behind My Darkness
by
Michael Tavon

Whatever you choose, you are somebody.
Live life to the fullest until you leave
This earth empty.
Navigate with empathy;
You will never feel lost.

Find your true self and stand proud
On your achievements and mistakes.
When someone tries to tell you how to live,
Ask them, *have you found your way yet?*
Most likely, they have not.

This life belongs to you
Always start with your heart
No matter where you go
You will always end with love

The Beauty Behind My Darkness
by
Michael Tavon

A Song for You

Have you ever heard
A song so beautiful
That it made you cry
But you didn't know why?

So you just kept playing
As the tears went by…

Have you ever heard of a
Tune that was so sweet that made
You feel so alive
That you forgot how to die?

So you just kept singing,
Singing till the sun said goodnight.

Play that song,
Play that song,
Til you no longer feel alone.

Sing along,
Sing along,
All the way home.

Please don't run,
Don't run away
When this song plays.
This song will brighten your day.

Feel what you need,
Crying is okay.

Don't turn it down,
Listen 'til the pain fades.
Turn up the bass
And shake your worries away.

The Beauty Behind My Darkness
by
Michael Tavon

Stress is just a phase,
Dance till your feet
Sweep those troubles away.

Angst is just a phrase.
Sing this song,
Till your voice becomes
A parade.

Play this song,
Play this song
Till you no longer feel alone.

Sing along,
Sing along
All the way home.

The Beauty Behind My Darkness
by
Michael Tavon

War & Leisure: Duplex

America is a dark home scarred by war.
I loathe violence; I was born to love.

I was born to love; war is a lazy resolve.
It's easier to fight until nothing remains.

Nothing but charred remains after the war.
Love is all I have to call my own.

Love is all I have to call my own,
I will protect this heart at all costs.

I will protect this heart at all costs,
Even if that means war.

I'll go to war for what I love,
This country was built on blood and tears.

This country was built on blood and tears;
America is a dark home scarred by war.

The Beauty Behind My Darkness
by
Michael Tavon

Post-break up

Allow the hurt to do its work, then let it go.
The memories will cut deep, and blood will seep
Through the patches, but time will stitch those
wounds.
After the pain subsides, use this space to clear your
Mind and realign with who you were before the
storm.
Don't waste your energy seeking closure from the
Abuser who tried to break you.
The answers you seek are within;
External validation isn't required.
Your past doesn't deserve a reservation to your
future.
Absolve that pain;
 Evolve and then walk away.

The Beauty Behind My Darkness
by
Michael Tavon

8.2.17

I just got kissed
By a raindrop.
I pray this pleasure
Never stops
Smoking leaves
From the maple tree,
And getting high so naturally.

Living a life in solitude,
The sky is wide
And I'm far from blue.
I see the truth.
I'm better off without you.

The Beauty Behind My Darkness
by
Michael Tavon

Long Distance Friendship

I have a long-distance
Friendship with depression.
We're not as close
As we used to be.
To be perfectly honest,
I'm allayed, it's no longer
Within arm's reach.
The proximity between us
Is a thousand football fields away.
When depression asks to stay,
I bluntly say, "Remain where you lay."
There's no way in hell I'm letting
It crowd my space again
Because depression never comes alone.
It always brings delusion
And drama for fun.
I refuse to party with them;
I'd stay in my happy home.
I'm content with the distance.
There's no need for us
To be close again.

The Beauty Behind My Darkness
by
Michael Tavon

A Heart to Heart with My Inner-Child

I'm sorry I sheltered you for so long.
I was protecting you from a somber side of me
and didn't want you to get harmed.
It's not your fault, I was ashamed,
Running from my shadow in the dark.
I thought it would be best for us
to take some time apart.

You didn't need to see your superhero
in a vulnerable position. (At least I thought)
When I heard your footsteps running
in my direction, I created more distance.

You didn't deserve to be deserted,
I made you feel more worthless
because I was hurting,
which wasn't my intention or purpose.

After pushing you away, I realized;
I only felt empty because you were no longer
a part of me. Instead of treating you
like a strength, I made you a liability.

Leaving you behind was a grave mistake.
I'm glad I realized before it was too late.
Please forgive me for dissing you when I needed
your help; because I'm still trying to forgive myself.

The Beauty Behind My Darkness
by
Michael Tavon

The Ultimatum

Your dreams are a reflection of you,
So, when the person you love
Doesn't believe, that means
They can't see into the mirror of your soul.

If you don't let them go
You'll be stuck in a hamster wheel
Of trying to prove them wrong.
It will be the same old song
When they say, "I told you so."

When things don't go right,
The doubts, the cries, the fights,
They won't understand why you stay up
Late at night, they'll fight tooth and nail
To dim your light.

Your dream is who you truly are
When no one is around.
It keeps you alive,
It gives you an inspiring high.

When the person
You share your body with
Tries to take that away
It's not tough love,
It's emotional homicide.

The Beauty Behind My Darkness
by
Michael Tavon

A Guide on How I Fell in Love with Myself

On a sunny afternoon,
I held deep conversations
With myself over brunch and mimosas.
 I didn't care if I appeared lonesome.
Solo dates were often wholesome.

Then I'd go to the theater,
Catch a film, or hit the gym.

Stroll to the record place,
Cop some Marvin Gaye,
Fleetwood, Mayfield,
 I'd lose track of time
Digging through the $5 crates.

Then I'd head to the bookstore
For vintage novels, Bukowski,
Angelou, if they had them, I got them.

If I had an hour to spare
I'd book a massage,
To relieve my stress without a care.

After a long day of treating myself
To the day I deserved
I went home,
Smoked a joint,
Played video games.
And fell asleep.

When I fell in awe with dating myself,
Each day felt like a blessing,
Not a burden.

The Beauty Behind My Darkness
by
Michael Tavon

A Declaration

My mind flooded with intrusive impulses
Engulfed by the ugliest side of me,
In an ocean of carnal pleasure
I chase short-term highs over sobriety.
I don't recognize this
Version of my skin;
Stripped naked of my innocence,
I only see the scars from sin.

My intuition is an army
Of one with no guns
Fighting against a nation
Of unholy lust.
In whom should I trust?
I'm stronger than any urge.
I will deal with them all
Until they burn to dust.

I refuse to lose,
I am stronger than I was.
I will not succumb;
The real battle has just begun.

The Beauty Behind My Darkness
by
Michael Tavon

The Today and Now

I'm not a psychic,
I can't see into the future.
I'm not a time traveler,
I can't alter the past.

Today is a gift that belongs to me,
Yesterday will not take this away,
And tomorrow needs to wait for the
Sun to arrive again.

I will treasure the present,
The most fascinating gift
Anyone could receive.
Many people didn't survive yesterday
The way I did.
I'm a lucky one.

I will not waste this
Blessing chasing after
Moments that aren't
Meant to be held captive.

Lifetime of Smiles

I hope the next person you open your heart to,
Knows how to handle it with care.
You don't deserve another heartbreak.
I hope they cleanse your spirit with endless
Affirmations because the people you trust treat you
Like a stranger behind your back.
You need someone to reassure you.
You are glorious.
When that person arrives in your life,
I hope you won't reject the blessing before your eyes.
You deserve to find your lifetime of smiles.

The Beauty Behind My Darkness
by
Michael Tavon

Galaxy

Your mind is a galaxy
With constellations, planets,
Retrogrades, and moons.

It's too vast to contain,
Too complex to understand,
Too gorgeous to ignore,
And too limitless to settle for less.

When someone says your dreams
Aren't realistic, don't keep them
In your orbit.

Life is too short to keep
Unsupportive people in your space.

The Beauty Behind My Darkness
by
Michael Tavon

Deserving

I deserve a love that accepts
Every version of me.
I don't want to be judged
For the mistakes, I've evolved from.

I deserve a love that will help
Protect my inner child.
It's the only side of me
That hasn't been tainted.

I deserve a love that allows me to be free.
This soft heart was constrained
By a tough love once before.

I deserve a love
That's air to my wings.
I don't want to be suffocated
By envy or pity.

I deserve this type of love,
It's the esoteric reverence I need
Because it's the love I will provide
When it finds me.

The Beauty Behind My Darkness
by
Michael Tavon

New Growth II

When a little hope remains,
Keep it in a safe space
Near your heart.
Don't let anything
Take it away.

When the smoke clears
And your old life has faded
Into dust,
That last seed of hope
Is all you will need to plant
Into the soil to harvest new growth.

The Beauty Behind My Darkness
by
Michael Tavon

New Season

After all the hardship and headaches,
I'm finally entering a new season.

I feel the relief chilling through my bones.
I feel the growth sprouting from my soul.

I'm so immersed in discovering a higher self.
I no longer indulge in a life
that once tried to break me.

I'm infatuated with the process
Of shedding the error of my ways.

The next time I step outside of my shell
I will be refined and in tune
With the atmosphere around me.

My inner child deserves a hug.
My teen self deserves to be heard.
My young adult self deserves forgiveness.
My present self deserves to be loved
Unconditionally.

This is my season.
I claim it.
I own it.

The Beauty Behind My Darkness
by
Michael Tavon

Puzzles

Your person needs to be the missing piece
To the puzzle of your life,
And you must be the same for them.

When you try to force a bond that doesn't fit,
It will be a constant, tug and pull to make it work.

You can't mold someone into being
The perfect fit for you,
As no one can squeeze you into
A space you don't belong.

Instead of trying to jam
A square peg into a circle
Exercise patience until the right piece
Comes into your life.
You'll know because they'll
Effortlessly fall into place.

No toil will be vital for bliss,
The right love will be a seamless fit.

The Beauty Behind My Darkness
by
Michael Tavon

Locked Up

They inflicted the most pain.
Your heart has endured
But have the audacity to ask
If you two can remain friends.

Do what's best for you
By denying them access
To your space.
Change the locks
And never give them
The key to your heart again.

The Beauty Behind My Darkness
by
Michael Tavon

A Hard Head Makes a Soft...

Sometimes we create our own mess,
Then complain about cleaning it up.

Sometimes we conjure our own storms,
Then weep over a lack of sun.

Sometimes we shoot ourselves
In the foot, then beg God
To give us strength
To walk again.

Sometimes we feed the body toxins,
Then blame cancer for our organs rotting.

Hardheaded people are often
Too arrogant to listen to the wiser minds
And too blind to see the truth.

We tend to blame the world
For the self-inflicted pain,
When we could've too learned
Our lesson without the suffering.

The Beauty Behind My Darkness
by
Michael Tavon

Tanka

You can't spell evolve.
Without love, you may plant seeds
But growth is futile.
Love requires light and honesty
To realize its potential.

The Beauty Behind My Darkness
by
Michael Tavon

A Quick Rant about Love

Love doesn't require pain.
Love doesn't require struggle.
Love doesn't require sacrifice.
Social conditioning has taught a generation
That heartache and love go hand in hand.
Love will shield you from the obstacles of life,
Not put you in harm's way.
Love is romance without apologies.

It's soft,
Compassionate,
Empathetic,
Passionate,
And liberating.

Real love doesn't kill the most authentic parts of you. Real love will never make you abuse your morals to Keep your partner happy, Nor will it force you into uncomfortable situations. Never become a hostage to toxicity for love's sake.

The Beauty Behind My Darkness
by
Michael Tavon

***Hardheaded...*本**

I'm too hardheaded to give up on myself
Even when my conscience urges me to.
Living to die is a waste of time.
I must finish what I started.

I arrived on this land,
Of oceans and mountains
For reasons unknown,
But this body was built
To swim and climb
To conquer this life.
It's a birthright.

These hands were made
To love and fight,
But not to fight the people I love.

Life is a gamble.
When I shuffle my deck,
Giving up isn't in the cards.

I'm eager to see what's on the horizon.
My curiosity will lead me,
Not kill me.

The Beauty Behind My Darkness
by
Michael Tavon

Mental Diet

My mind is exhausted:
Out of shape,
It gets winded
After a marathon
Of overthinking.

I try to pace this race
But my thoughts
Keep sprinting.

I need to slow down—
Find a steady pace
Clear this clutter
And create more mental space.

I can't blame social media
For being my choice of junk food.
I can't blame video games
For being my choice of drug.
I am my own enabler.

My mental diet
Needs to change
If I want to be
Here for the long haul.

The Beauty Behind My Darkness
by
Michael Tavon

Unexpected Guest II

When change introduces itself to you
Fear may whisper doubt into your ears
But listen to what change has to say.
Don't push it away.

Be warm and friendly.
Change is not the enemy.
The first encounter will be awkward
And its veracity will make your soul uneasy.

Change isn't always sweet on the eyes;
When standing face to face,
It can be an unpleasant sight,
But it's always worth getting to know.

So when change comes,
Be a tour guide
And explore the depths of your
Chilling past that made
Your skin cold.

It may hurt at first
To accept change,
But no strength is acquired
Without pain.

Change is an unexpected guest
But don't stress,
It's only the best friend
You haven't met yet.

The Beauty Behind My Darkness
by
Michael Tavon

A huge weight
Was lifted off my chest
The moment I forgave
The ones who tried to break me.

The Beauty Behind My Darkness
by
Michael Tavon

Before I Drown

I try my best to not stress over
The elements I can't control,
but I can't help but think,
What am I doing wrong?
Is it my fault?

Am I trying too hard to gain
something that doesn't want
To be in my possession?

These are the questions
constantly flooding my mind;
Hopefully, I'll find the strength
To swim to shore,
before I get drowned
by my thoughts.

The Beauty Behind My Darkness
by
Michael Tavon

*I'd rather be accepted
Into a small village of compassion than
To live in a city of wickedness.*

The Beauty Behind My Darkness
by
Michael Tavon

Note to self:

Even when your mind feels lost, your heart knows
The right way to go.
You've come a long way, why waste steps doubting
Yourself now?
Instead, allow your intuition to be your own North
Star. It hasn't steered you wrong yet.

The Beauty Behind My Darkness
by
Michael Tavon

Don't become so *reformed* that you forget who you were.
On the other hand, don't become so *self-righteous*
That you start judging people for the mistakes you once made.
Having a selective memory doesn't give you the right to act high and mighty.

The Beauty Behind My Darkness
by
Michael Tavon

A Message to a Friend

Life has been dealing punches
Too fast to counter,
You put your guard up
Till your arms grow tired.

I hope you're doing well

Pouring your heart Into the wrong cups
Leaves you thirstier for love
Than you were before

I hope you're doing well

Losing your resolve to do right
Wings too weak to take flight
Out of mind, and out of sight.
The struggle feels like a birthright.

I hope you're doing well

The same results;
The same mistakes,
You must be going insane.
When will you stare into the mirror
And make that change?
Don't wait till it's too late.

I hope you're doing well

The Beauty Behind My Darkness
by
Michael Tavon

Sonku

Love is where
The heart goes,
To grow old
Where the ego
Comes to die,
And where the
Soul stays young.

The Beauty Behind My Darkness
by
Michael Tavon

Lost Inner Child

There's a little one inside you
Who once dreamt of becoming
An astronaut, a professional athlete,
And a fashion model.

Your imagination
Ran wild through the backyard
As you envisioned yourself
Being… being larger than life…
Being someone beyond
Your ancestors' wildest dreams.

Those dreams were deferred
By the adults who told you that you could
Be nothing more than what they were.
That little child died
When they were told to not keep
Those dreams alive.

Now that little one
Is lost in the mundane,
Lost behind a desk, bills, and essays,
Wondering what could've been
And what should've been
If they were encouraged to believe
In the dreams, they had set to achieve.

The Beauty Behind My Darkness
by
Michael Tavon

Maybe it's You

When was the last time you looked inward and took
Accountability for your failed relationships?
What patterns did you repeat?
Where did you refuse to grow?
Your reflection can be haunting when you don't want
To see the truth, but you are the common
Denominator in all your relationships.
If all your relationships end the same, maybe, it's
Time for you to take some of the blame.
Maybe you're a victim of your own bad habits.

The Beauty Behind My Darkness
by
Michael Tavon

Let them go even if it makes you a villain in their story.
Never stop doing what feels right in your soul,
Because you fear being called ill-fitting names that don't suit you.
Their perception of you doesn't have to be your reality.

The Beauty Behind My Darkness
by
Michael Tavon

Final Words

Since tomorrow is never promised
Take the first opportunity to make amends.
Don't let anger and pride blind
You from seeing what's important.

Because if you get robbed of the chance
To say all the words, you wish to say,
For the rest of your days,
You'll be haunted by regret,
The regrets of not being able
To speak of them again.

The Beauty Behind My Darkness
by
Michael Tavon

You're Strong but Tired

The bags you carry under
Those eyes are overflowing
With stress.
Now is the time;
Unpack and gather some rest.

You try so hard to prove that fatigue
Isn't a weakness, because previous generations
Told us that tiredness is a disease
And the only cure is to work through it.

We watched our grandparents work
To their graves,
We've witnessed
Our parents work until their youth faded.
All they ever passed down was work,
That's all they had to give.
Work, work, work, work, work…
It's not just a catchy hook by Rihanna.
It consumes who you are,
Till it becomes your entire persona.

Overworked and stressed out,
Trying to prove to the world
That you are worth every breath
You take, but you are worth far more
Than the wage you make.

This can't be life,
All work and no rest
Makes you a zombie in living flesh.

The Beauty Behind My Darkness
by
Michael Tavon

The Big Catch

Today a wise man told me
"Life is like fishing,
You won't catch anything
Unless you try."

An epiphany struck like lightning
When those words seeped
Through my soul.

It takes a tremendous deal of
Humility, patience, and unwavering hope
To keep going when things don't
Flow in your direction.

Even when the waters
Are slow and bleak,
As the sky says goodbye to the sun,
You sit there with this belief
That something massive will
Tug the line.

They also require a strategy to succeed.
You have to know the best time,
The perfect tide,
And know which bait to use.
The same way,
(A dream without a plan,
Is just an aimless thought,
With passive effort)

It's always mundane and unpredictable
On any given day;
You never know what you're going to get
But won't get a damn thing
If you don't try.

The Beauty Behind My Darkness
by
Michael Tavon

The Slap

Don't assume
anything.
Get to know me
instead,
It's lazy to judge
someone
Based on rumors,
Through the grapevine.
If you're not willing
To learn me inside & out,
Keep my name
Out of your mouth.

The Beauty Behind My Darkness
by
Michael Tavon

Note to Self

You're down right now, but ***this season*** won't last forever.
Take this time to re-evaluate and refocus.
Fall back from the social life, you need to.
Like a caterpillar tucked inside its cocoon,
You don't have to show the world your process;
Just pop out, when it's time for your ***wings to flourish.***

The Beauty Behind My Darkness
by
Michael Tavon

Parasite Paradise

Some people will drag your trust through the mud
Because they know your loyalty won't budge.
As they do everything to drive you away,
You continue to keep them in your space.
Your heart is not big enough to tolerate
Their disrespect, time and time again.
Someday, it will break.
It's best to fade away from their ruinous space.
Never let those parasites make a paradise out of your kindness.

The Beauty Behind My Darkness
by
Michael Tavon

*You deserve **soul-cleansing sex**-*
*A **transformational love***
*And **broken generational curses**,*
So your true healing can commence.
I hope you let this soak in.

The Beauty Behind My Darkness
by
Michael Tavon

Gentle Reminder

Your heart has a ***drought of confidence***,
But this feeling is temporary.
So weed out those negative thoughts
And prune the thorns that stab your hands when You
reach for anything beautiful.
Stay the course;
Sometimes setbacks are essential
When you want your blessings to ***bloom abundantly***.

The Beauty Behind My Darkness
by
Michael Tavon

*Are they really a **soul tie** or are you shackled by the fantasies they sold you? When they say "I love you," do you feel liberated or imprisoned?*

The Beauty Behind My Darkness
by Michael Tavon

Half Empty

Waking up alone,
Doesn't feel as bad
As it seems.
Sometimes a mattress
Needs a break
From the extra weight.
Sometimes the body,
Needs a moment to breathe.
Sometimes the pillow
Needs a good cry.
Sometimes blankets
Get tired of hosting ghosts.
Is the bed half-empty
Or half full?
It depends…
Were the nights filled with love?
Were the days littered with lies?

The Beauty Behind My Darkness
by
Michael Tavon

Gentle Reminder

Love shouldn't have to be ***fought for***.
Nor should it ever ***feel like a contest***.
True love is not a reality dating show.
If you decide to stick around, they make
You look like a clown.
The cold, hard truth is that you carry some
blame for letting them make a ***fool of you.***

The Beauty Behind My Darkness
by
Michael Tavon

The Truest Form

"I only speak from two places: love and experience"

My tongue is far from misinformed.
You won't catch me speaking on subjects
I don't possess a grasp on.

If I never lived it or never took the time
To listen, I will hold my breath,
I won't be a waste of space
By giving baseless opinions.

My heart is my greatest gift.
I never set out to hurt anyone
When I tell them how I feel.
Everything I say is real.
I speak from love.
That's all I know.

Love will always be the answer.
Sometimes silence is love.
Listening is love.
Being present is love.

Sometimes I keep my mouth closed
And allow my heart to do the talking.

The Beauty Behind My Darkness
by
Michael Tavon

When my heart rains,
I remain optimistic,
Because I know,
After the storm subsides,
A stronger soul will emerge
From the wet soil.

The Beauty Behind My Darkness
by
Michael Tavon

Trim & Declutter

If your life is filled
With an excess
Of untrustworthy people,
It's time to declutter
Your inner circle.

The childish drama
They bring around
Is only bringing
You down.

Your loyalty is a crown.
Be aware of who you
Share it with,
Not everyone has the best intentions.

The Beauty Behind My Darkness
by
Michael Tavon

Sound Waves

On the frigid days
When the sun hangs
In the sky for decoration,
I gravitate to meditation,
To keep my balance.
The steel tongue drum,
The crystal sound bowl
With a mallet,
Or rolling the Baoding balls
In my palm,
So the vibration
Can sing to ears.

I do all I can to prevent myself
From sulking in the dull moments.
When the walls are closing
And my heart feels divided
These spiritual devices,
 Keep me whole and grounded.

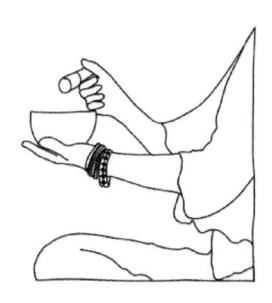

The Beauty Behind My Darkness
by
Michael Tavon

When your back
Is against the ropes
And an ounce of hope
Is all you have,
Fight for yourself.
You are worth the effort.

The Beauty Behind My Darkness
by
Michael Tavon

Nostalgic Highs

An ode to the beloved memories
That pleasantly haunt me:
They often remind me
The good ole days
Are worth savoring,
But it's dangerous
To reminisce for too long.
I must know when to let go,
So, I can create more space
For new memories to come.

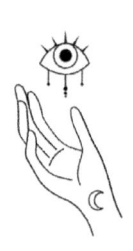

The Beauty Behind My Darkness
by
Michael Tavon

I know life has been rough, to say the least,
But please understand this, I got you.
And I'll provide you a shoulder to lean on
When you lack the strength to carry on.
I promise you don't have to move mountains alone.

The Beauty Behind My Darkness
by
Michael Tavon

Winter Moods: Prism

Harsh
Winter mood,
My heart dreams of June.
I long for the sun's tirade
As warm ray's parade on my pale skin.

Sun
Please come again.
A sweet summer rain,
Save me from this cruel cold wind.
Give me a chance to savor each day.

Love
Is my home
But I crave nature to
Smile bright from beyond those clouds.
My soul starves for your warmth,
I need you.

The Beauty Behind My Darkness
by
Michael Tavon

I Was Never Broken: Duplex

Healing is an avenue toward home.
I'll work on myself till I get there.

I will work on myself till home is fixed.
There's nothing these hands won't build.

These hands won't build a façade,
I refuse to live an illusion and call it love.

I once thought love was an illusion.
I took pretty lies over the ugly truth.

The truth gets too ugly to sit with alone.
I prayed for refuge when my heart got lost.

I found the refuge my heart longed for,
Healing is an avenue toward home.

The Beauty Behind My Darkness
by
Michael Tavon

Misdemeanor

The world is full of
Judges with no gavels,
Lawyers with no practice
And prisons with no bars.
Minor misdemeanors
Lead to the demise
Of precious time.
Forgiveness isn't free
When the world
Treats your life like a crime.

The Beauty Behind My Darkness
by
Michael Tavon

To the Troll Who Called Me a Narcissist for Loving Myself

I get wrongfully judged for the amount of love I pour into myself. They call me Ill-fitting words in an attempt to snap my spirit in half, but their opinions aren't strong enough to break me. I love myself loud and unapologetically. Self-love is viewed as voodoo to the wicked spirits that hate to see anyone happy. My confidence is seen as obscene to eyes that lack the depth to perceive my story. It took a lifetime to feel this good about waking up. My soul is soft and warm, shame no longer burns holes through my skin when I stare at my reflection. Pride hangs from my neck like a medal. No Geppetto can put me on a string, I control my own destiny. I'm not arrogant, self-centered, a narcissist or whatever buzzword they throw like stones to shatter the windows of my happy home. They want to humble me like my confidence is a disease, but why? They never inquire about how I got here. They never take the time to learn how I went from feeling worse than worthless to defining my purpose. Self-love is a journey some people rush to judge without a court; because they're too lazy to understand the work that goes into loving myself.

The Beauty Behind My Darkness
by Michael Tavon

11.6.16

No one has
More power over
Your life than you.

When you stare into the mirror
And see fear and doubt,
Glaring back at you,
Remember
It's all in your head.
Nothing is more beautiful
Than self-confidence.

Remember you're a mosaic of flaws
With room for improvement.
Never deem yourself unworthy
For being short of perfection.

The Beauty Behind My Darkness
by
Michael Tavon

Reshaping: Duplex

Love is reshaping dark clouds into glory,
A gentle nudge toward my silver lining.

My silver lining shone after heavy rain.
I've come to appreciate the beauty in pain.

The pain is only appreciated in retrospect,
But it's the worst gift in present time.

In the present time, I place the memories
In a glass case as a display of my mistakes.

I display my mistakes with no shame,
Only through the pain, I learned how to love.

I learned how to love through the pain I endured,
My heart beats softer than ever before.

My heart beats softer than ever before.
Love reshaped my dark clouds into glory.

The Beauty Behind My Darkness
by
Michael Tavon

The Storm: Duplex

My heart beats softer than ever before,
Love reshaped my dark clouds into glory.

Depression was a dark cloud eager to pour.
My first love was a storm I wasn't ready for.

I wasn't ready; my first love was a storm,
And with no umbrella, I couldn't stand the rain.

I couldn't stand the rain; a sad song for us.
It was a new edition of heartbreak if it wasn't love.

If it wasn't love, why did a piece of me die
When it was time to finally let go?

When it was time to let go, I transformed
From a boy to a man, at the end of our road.

Although we've come to the end of the road.
My heart beats softer than ever before.

The Beauty Behind My Darkness
by
Michael Tavon

Kiss The Sky: Duplex

Now I've come to the end of the road,
My heart beats softer than ever before.

My heart beats softer than a pillow.
I rest my head on a cloud when I kiss the sky.

When I kiss the sky, confetti falls like rain.
I celebrate my freedom like a newborn.

Like a newborn, fresh air feels liberating,
After thriving in a crowded loneliness.

I thrived in a crowded loneliness.
There's nothing in this life I can't handle.

There's nothing in this life I can't handle;
When a lane closes, I pave a new path.

I pave a path more promising than the past.
 It's the end of the road; I'm never coming back.

The Beauty Behind My Darkness
by
Michael Tavon

Ask a Better Question, Please

When people ask,
"What do you do for work?"
My tongue hides behind my teeth,
Because my truth is used to being misunderstood.
Then a long pause and deep breaths creates a thin
layer of tension.

Whenever I answer
It's often met with vague facial expressions
And condescending follow ups;
"Is that sustainable?"
"What's next?"
" do you actually make money?"
(while some people are actually nice tho)

I loathe being asked what I do for work,
because work and I never got along
I've quit over 20 jobs in my life.

So, if you really want to know ask
"What do you do for life?"
I'll tell you, I pour hope into the world,
I crack my heart open, so everyone can
See what's inside, I build worlds out of words
I make the impossible seem normal.

The Beauty Behind My Darkness
by
Michael Tavon

Work Life

When most people gather
they talk about
what they have most in common *work,*
they complain about their bosses
They rant about the coworker
Who is always late
They spill the tea on break room gossip.
I just sit idly wondering why
People escape work to devout
Their free time and energy
Talking about the thing they loathe the most,
But it's not their fault
So many people spend so much of their time
At work that it's become a second home,
They've forgotten what makes them smile,
What makes them feel alive.
Work is all they have to talk about
I urge you to find the thing that
Makes you feel wild,
The thing that makes you feel free,
The think that makes you smile
Don't spend your life dying behind a 9-5,
You deserve to feel alive,
You deserve to find that slice of life
That ignites a light so bright
The atmosphere shines when
You part your lips to talk about it

The Beauty Behind My Darkness
by
Michael Tavon

The Key to Feeling Good

A small act of kindness,
Has the power to unlock
The joy inside a heart
That's chained by anguish,

Don't hesitate to say something nice
When it crosses your mind,
A sweet compliment could last a mile
When it travels to the ears of those
Who need hear your pleasant words the most

Compassion has a lasting effect
When you have enough to spare
Today is the perfect day to show
How much you care

Make this world a brighter place;
Every smile is a poem
Composed of meaningful words

The art of kindness Is a gift that gives
Everyone the chance to create
Something wondrous

The Beauty Behind My Darkness
by
Michael Tavon

Section III

My Love is the Sun

The Beauty Behind My Darkness
by
Michael Tavon

Like an Interview

Love can be dangerous.
So I protect myself.
Are you good for my heart
Or bad for my mental health?

I've been down this road,
Hit a curb & took a wrong turn.
Now will you be a blessing
Or a lesson learned?

I'm not trying to pay
For mistakes your ex made.
Are you healed from his shit
Or will I go into debt?

I got baggage,
I never claimed to be perfect.
Will you love my flaws
Or deem me worthless?

I know I'm asking 21 questions
Like an interview.
I'm just trying to dig deep
Because I'm feeling you.

Now Tell me your love language,
And past trauma.
Do you get daddy issues
Or mama drama?

The Beauty Behind My Darkness
by
Michael Tavon

See, the key to love
Is trust and empathy.
Can I unlock a part of you
To see if we match mentally?

All, I got a dollar and a dream.
I'll split it 50-50,
Only if you're willing to support
And believe in me

The Beauty Behind My Darkness
by
Michael Tavon

You Wanting Me Too

You wanting me as much
as I want you sounds kinda crazy, maybe,
but I've been dealing with a lot of rejection lately
My mind hazy with doubt
Wondering if we were to fall in love
Would we work out or lose all the muscle
If love is dangerous are you worth the trouble
No more struggle, I deserve a soft love ,
Because I'm attracted to your empathy
I'm healing from the side effects
Of my exes—could you be the remedy
It's hard to believe that you're feeling me
I get jittery when you speak, it's only been a week
but We have a connection on the horizon
stronger than Verizon's
I don't wanna move too fast
But there's an uprising inside of me,
You're guiding me, telling me to follow this
surprise; you came into my life so sudden(ly)
The start of something
Didn't have a chance to prepare.
I didn't see you coming…
But I'm not gonna run and leave with nothing
Just being Frank in this ocean
Under the wind let's see how this beginning will end
Will we become new lovers or old friends..
A story only time will tell
As we write these chapters in pen
I want you, you want me. I shouldn't doubt that all
The way you look at me
Makes my worries seem so small

The Beauty Behind My Darkness
by
Michael Tavon

If I got down on one knee,
Took you by the hand
And asked,
"Would you spend
The rest of your life with me?
What would you say?"

The Beauty Behind My Darkness
by
Michael Tavon

White Dress: Duplex

When I envision you in a white dress,
 Butterflies arise inside my mind like fire.

My mind becomes a fire I refuse to put out
Because you are my only and final flame.

My final flame let's burn for eternity.
I'm so eager to call you my wife.

I will call you my wife and celebrate.
The confetti in my heart is ready and set.

My heart is set on you like the sun at dusk,
The most gorgeous sight to behold.

I behold the most gorgeous sight
When I envision you in a white dress

The Beauty Behind My Darkness
by
Michael Tavon

Can't Take My Eyes off You

Are we living
In a dream world?
A love like this
Feels too surreal, girl
Since the first time
You said *I love you,*
 I've been pinching myself
To make sure
It's really you.

The Beauty Behind My Darkness
by
Michael Tavon

Triple Haiku

As time passes by,
Our love will age like fine wine.
We savor each day,

Pour our memories
Till the rivers overflow
And sip nirvana.

Forever is near;
Growing old is a blessing,
As we age like wine.

The Beauty Behind My Darkness
by
Michael Tavon

Dreamers: Duplex

As midnight gently matures into the day,
It feels like a dream sleeping next to you.

When I sleep next to you,
My thoughts don't welter into nightmares.

I would toss and turn through nightmares;
Now I am lucky to have you by my side.

To have you by my side
Is visual proof that heaven is real.

Heaven is real; I'm elated.
Life is taking its time with you and me.

Life takes its precious time with you and me
As midnight gently matures into dawn.

The Beauty Behind My Darkness
by
Michael Tavon

After "I Do"

Some say love becomes
A chore after marriage,
And vows decompose
Into words etched in stone
As death becomes a daily practice.
I was made to believe marriage
Is a forced habit of fake happiness,
A mere business transaction for taxes
Forever stuck in the age of worry,
A suffering that lasts
As the imagination remains stagnant.
I have faith, our bond
Will grow after matrimony.
Let our laugh lines over time
Be a testimony
As we author a new story
Of all the good times
Our hearts will share.
We start with love; hoping it ends there.

The Beauty Behind My Darkness
by
Michael Tavon

Songs for Her Mood I: Michael Jackson

You give me *butterflies*,
Every time you *smile*.
I'm *speechless* when you
Say *baby be mine*,

The *lady of my life*,
Till the day I die
But *heaven can wait*.
On this earth, I have to stay
Each day I pray
That you will never *fly away*.

Because *you are not alone*
My *P.Y.T.*, please *give into me*.
There's nothing in these *hot streets*
But *Dirty Diana's* and *Billie Jeans*.
The way you make me feel
Makes me wanna *scream,*
The girl is mine. I can't help it,
 But remember the time
You rocked my world,
And said, *you are my lif*e.

With my heart on a *carousel,*
You spin me.
 I'm a *slave to the rhythm*
Of your heartbeat.
I feel a good kind of weak
When you speak to me.

The Beauty Behind My Darkness
by
Michael Tavon

I got to be there.
I wanna be where you are.
My feelings for you are *off the wall.*

Baby, *I just can't stop loving you,*
I wouldn't even if I could
Cuz got damn; *love never felt so good.*

The Beauty Behind My Darkness
by
Michael Tavon

Your smile is my motivation,
An indication I'm doing right
By you.

The Beauty Behind My Darkness
by
Michael Tavon

No Brainer

We all know,
Adele can move the mountains
In our hearts, when she sings,
And Ed Sheeran
Will make love seem like
The perfect day that never ends
With his pen.

We all know Viola Davis
Will make you feel
Like you're in the same room,
When she delivers her lines.

Without a doubt, these
Are things we all know right.
Like day will turn to night,
And our hair will turn grey
As each strand celebrates
The passing of time …

We all know Friends
Ripped off Living Single,
And life itself will eventually end.

We all know O.J. did it,
Michael Jackson is innocent
And we shouldn't add cornstarch
To hot liquid.

There are universal truths
We can't change.
There's nothing we can do
And me spending
The rest of my life with you
Is a no-brainer too.

The Beauty Behind My Darkness
by
Michael Tavon

Whenever, Wherever, Whatever (2023)

Take samples of my heart.
Slow the chords; love is a song,
Listen to me whenever you feel lost.

I love you for all that you are.
Wherever you go, I will not be far.
I belong to you; I am yours,
Whenever, wherever, whatever.

Stare into these eyes, you'll see my soul.
My love is the flow.
Be with the rhythm,
We will float to wherever you need to go.

If it is the air that you need,
Strum my lungs till you breathe.
Whatever you ask baby,
I will be whenever,
Wherever,
And whatever.

Sing this love like a falsetto.
Let me be the warm song
You play when your soul feels cold.

I'll play however you want.
I only yearn to be yours,
Whenever,
Wherever,
And whatever.

The Beauty Behind My Darkness
by
Michael Tavon

Her Favorite Color (sonnet)

Sweet like a fresh batch of lemonade,
With the warm aura of a summer sun,
I swim in the calm heat; never run for shade.
Living in a dream, a new life begins.
When her legs split wide like banana peels,
And my hand on her skin,
A flame slowly burns.
She's eager to see how my nature feels.
I can't get enough; my body yearns for her.
A sight to behold as her dearest rose,
Her sunlight smile brings life into my eyes.
My grey sky turned gold, so bright I suppose,
She is truth in a world colored with lies,
The mother of her favorite color,
The birth of joy, a vibe like no other.

The Beauty Behind My Darkness
by
Michael Tavon

Tanka

Would you wear my last
Name, till the hues fade to grey
And the seams grow weak
From holding fabric too long?
Love never goes out of style.

The Beauty Behind My Darkness
by
Michael Tavon

Please Excuse My Dear Aunt Sally

Love isn't an equation,
Don't make it complicated.
It's joy x consistency + good conversation.

Never jaded by lazy days,
Take away (-) the frustrations,
That Jody & Yvette love is a little outdated.

We'll never get ÷ by white lies,
And lonely hours, I live to see you smile.

And trust to the ³ with two hearts of gold
By the touch of Midas, I only wanna+
To your peace, neve subtract any (minor problems);
That shall find us,
I promise we'll solve them.

No calculators are required,
Everything we desire will be acquired
Through patience x faith.
At the end of each day,
We'll be each other's safe space.

Us/the world is a beautiful fraction
Because no matter what happens,
You'll have my arms to wrap in.

Because love is so sublime,
Me + You = a connection
That's ahead of its time.

The Beauty Behind My Darkness
by
Michael Tavon

Songs for Her Mood: Miguel's Groove

Like *candles in the sun*
My flame will never burn out
You're my *sure thing*
whenever my mind gets clouded with doubt

You hit the spot like hot *coffee*
You got me higher than *pineapple skies*
Time flies like a *quickie*, skin covered in hickies

I'm falling like *leaves* in September,
remember to *face the sun*
When you look for me,

All I want is you
Girls like you are rare to find,
Those feet must've
Jogged through my mind
a thousand miles

Let my love *adorn* you *to the moon,*
My *Girl with the tattoo*
I get such a *thrill* when you
Come through and chill a feeling so real,

I feel anointed when you *arch & point*
what's the point in chasing
The fast life when the *simple things*
feels much better.

They say *what's the fun in forever*
But I've found the pleasure in knowing
You would never *use me*
In a bad way, let 'em tell it
This the life I wanna live
Til our *beautiful exit*

The Beauty Behind My Darkness
by
Michael Tavon

Body Smile

When the weight of the world
Lands on your shoulders,
I will relieve the stress
With my firm but gentle hands.

When another migraine attacks
Your brain, I will rub the pain,
Until the headache runs away
Like a brush to a canvas,
My fingers are like magic.

When your feet sore after a long day
Of walking through the store,
I will rub the stress from each toe.

When those cramps
Feel like an eruption
In your stomach, and the bloat
Intensifies like a summer sun,
I will unravel each knot
With my palms.

Whatever pain you may feel,
My hands will always
Find ways to make your body smile.

The Beauty Behind My Darkness
by
Michael Tavon

My Lady, My Dream

Your feet must be tired
From crossing my mind all-day,
My lady, my dream.
The voices in my head
Are telling me to pursue you,
Something they finally agree on.

What do I have to lose?
If you were to turn me away,
I'd probably lose more,
If I refrain from saying a thing.

One day,
My worries will pour
Into a well of courage.
So, I can profess the way
My heart is set on you.

I don't want to waste
Any more precious hours
Waiting for the perfect time
To sweep you off your feet.

The Beauty Behind My Darkness
by
Michael Tavon

My lady, my dream,
One day, my eyes will rise
With the sun.
I will stretch and scratch
My man parts.

And your voice will be
The first sound of my day.
Even as you lie next to me,
You will still be
My lady, my dream.

The Beauty Behind My Darkness
by
Michael Tavon

When a Poem Was All I Could Afford to Give

Each word seeped
Through the crevices of your mind.
So, whenever you thought of me,
Your body smiled.

When a poem was the only gesture
My wallet could afford,
You treated each metaphor
Like diamonds you adored.

You never made me feel poor
For being unable to afford
What (I thought) you deserved.
(To you), the handwritten poems
Neatly folded in your purse
Were golden nuggets to your heart.

Not hedging my bets, going all in
Left me in an emotional debt,
When the jackpot wasn't hit,
Broken time and time again.

But you never made me feel worthless
As I wrote beautiful verses in cursive
Ink spilled heartfelt moments,
Engraved on the surface
Of our hearts, no bank can disperse
The sum of wealth, these words
Have earned.

The Beauty Behind My Darkness
by
Michael Tavon

Imperfect II

Babe, I love you
With my whole heart,
Not just a piece.
When I see you,
There is beauty
Behind your darkness,
Like pouring rain
On a balmy day.
You're imperfect
In all the right ways.

The Beauty Behind My Darkness
by
Michael Tavon

There's Something Different about Me
Because of You

When I see old faces,
They recognize my new smile.
The room gets brighter,
And the atmosphere feels lighter.

They see the happiness
Glowing from my pores.
A colorful aura,
Radiates from my soles.

When they say,
"You look so happy, full of purpose,"
I never hesitate to
Credit my favorite person.

The world feels the rapture
Through each moment, we capture,
My posture no longer slouched
I stand taller in stature.

Family, friends, and old flings
See why you got the ring.
There's no doubt: my smile sings
You are my sure thing.

The Beauty Behind My Darkness
by
Michael Tavon

Naturally You

You say it's rare
For a man to want to see you
When your face is bare
With unkempt hair and no mascara,
And when you stare,
Well, I don't care.

I want to see the beauty
Of you when you wake up
Without the fake lashes
And makeup.
Let's lay up
And be lazy, with your hair
All tangled and wavy
In your grey sweats
From Old Navy baby.

To you, this sounds crazy or foreign.
You think the natural you is boring,
I think it's worth exploring.

Let me take a tour of your
Stretch marks and dimples.
Baby, it's not an issue.
I like it better when you're simple.
You give more while doing less.

I must confess,
I love how you can switch
From glam to natural.

The Beauty Behind My Darkness
by
Michael Tavon

From Friday sexy to Sunday casual,
It's admiral.

I love you naturally.
It's irrational to think
Makeup is the armor
That will guard you from harm.

I promise, to love each pimple
And scar.
Show me who you truly are.
Put me in awe, bare and all.
Naturally, you're special,
Naturally, you are…

The Beauty Behind My Darkness
by
Michael Tavon

Sonku

As rain sweeps,

Hold me close

'Tween the sheets.

Fill my bones

With comfort,

Thunder sings.

The Beauty Behind My Darkness
by
Michael Tavon

**ic The Fading Darkness*

At times I sit in disbelief
That this beautiful human
Is thrilled to marry all of me.
Not just the pieces she took apart
And decided to keep,
Not the potential;
She was wise enough
 To invest in me when the value was low,
But every last drop of me.
Her smile is the moon
To the fading darkness
In my heart.
When she envisions
Our special day,
Her eyes become a sea.
I waded through the coldest waters
To make it to my lady.
I'm so ready to add Mrs
To her name.
I can't believe someone like her
Is eager to wear my ring
Like a badge of honor.

*My greatest vow is to love her unconditionally
through every phase of me.*

The Beauty Behind My Darkness
by
Michael Tavon

A Question with No Answer

When you asked
"Where would you be if we never met?"

Most days felt bleak before your arrival.
My weary heart—weak,
Inner voices became rivals,
Life was a novel without a title,
Desperate for a tender touch.
I used sex as a crutch
And didn't care much
About tomorrow, but obsessed
With the yesterdays.
I couldn't wave goodbye.
The path I was headed
Wasn't a scenic view.
So, where would I be without you?
Lucky for me,
The answer will never come true.

The Beauty Behind My Darkness
by
Michael Tavon

Everlasting

You mourn for the love that died.
Your heart is war-torn but let me adorn you.
No sojourn: my love is everlasting.

Without asking, I'll shower your days
With the praise, you deserve to bask in.
No masking: I will always be real.

Peel back each layer,
Until you fathom how I feel.
If honesty is the way to your heart,
Let me take the wheel, so I can guide you.

By your side, I won't leave you behind.
If you open your eyes, you will see new life.
Love can't be in the dark,
We all need some sunshine.

The Beauty Behind My Darkness
by
Michael Tavon

Tanka

Does your body smile
When I jaunt your fantasies?
Loud snores shake the room
As we dream of sweet love,
Till the birds interrupt us.

The Beauty Behind My Darkness
by
Michael Tavon

New Lips to Kiss

I found new lips to kiss,
I hope they make a home on my skin
And stay for the rest of my life.

Her sweet lips give
A sugar high when we kiss.
I never wanna come down.

Her lips feel right,
I never felt a kiss like this
Had to be something
For me to write this.

All too common,
I'm often left falling
For someone who eventually
Stops calling,
But she feels different.

Kissing her lips
My new favorite verb.
They say everything
I need to hear
Without saying a word.

The Beauty Behind My Darkness
by
Michael Tavon

The Light (verse)

A love like yours
Isn't too common.
Women like you
Don't come around often.
You got my temp rising
Like water for chocolate.
I promise I get aroused by your power.
I confess, I climax
Before you even undress,
But between us,
I feel something
Deeper than sex.
The way our bodies connect
Has a spiritual effect,
A beautiful simplicity,
That's so complex.
I sent God a thank you text,
For giving everything
I prayed for.
Baby, you're all that I prayed for,
And so much more.
I never have wonder
My Cherie Amour,
Like Stevie, I sing
In the key of life.
When it's dark inside,
You are my light;
My Moonchild.
Like my intuition,
Your soul feels right.

The Beauty Behind My Darkness
by
Michael Tavon

The Light (verse II)

Your love is honey, it never spoils.
I get hot flashes of giving
You back shots with the recoil.
Your love is the light of my soul
 And the water to my soil.

When I'm digging you like a garden,
I plant food for thought
And watch our dreams
Grow for harvest.
We never starve,
We're forever evolving.
I honor the path you walk in.

The closest to heaven
I've ever been, is next to you.
It's a flex to be sexing you
Like good food;
I always want seconds, boo.

Digga-da, digga-da, digga-da, digga-digga-da-da!
You leave me tongue-tied
And speechless.
I hope I'll make you smile
When you see this, peace.

The Beauty Behind My Darkness
by
Michael Tavon

*When illness visits your body,
I will be by your side.
Until the virus vacates your sinuses,
I'll guide us back to health.
You will never have to fight a sickness
By yourself.*

The Beauty Behind My Darkness
by
Michael Tavon

Songs for Her Mood II: Jhene Aiko

Your love sends me
Higher than *sativa,*
And hotter than a fever.

Such a beautiful *trip,*
 In your *frequency,*
Frequently sends my mind
Into a dream without sleepin'

On this *mystic journey,*
We've found *a new balance*
Through passion.
It's a God-given talent.

When we love, it feels like *ascension,*
Giving what our spirits have been missing.
We frame this life with the *perfect picture,*
Creating new *moments to remember.*

You drift through my *spotless mind.*
When I close my eyes.
It feels like we're
The *only lovers left alive.*

Under *eternal sunshine*
While we're young.
Let's *surrender* our *sailing souls,*
Until we meet *the mourning doves.*

The Beauty Behind My Darkness
by
Michael Tavon

Omnipresent

It was a dream when I met you
My omnipresent angel
With crystal eyes shining bright
Every time you came through
Nothing less than beautiful
Your presence is a present
Now my present is so fruitful.

The Beauty Behind My Darkness
by
Michael Tavon

Moon's Muse

Infatuated by her mind,
I'm fixed on how she speaks.

The excitement in her eyes,
And the curl of her lips,
When she expresses her passions,
Causes sparks to arise of inside me.

She's the muse of a crescent moon.
She's why butterflies bloom
From cocoons.

I love the way she thinks.
She doesn't believe in limitations.
With her beautiful imagination,
Everything she envisions
Is a manifestation that comes true.

The power of her mind
Can part seas,
Move mountains,
And revive a dead forest.

Maybe I'm exaggerating,
But I wouldn't put it past her.
She's a dreamer, with a beautiful mind.
I'm proud to call her mine.

The Beauty Behind My Darkness
by
Michael Tavon

Someone to Trust

Going through the motions,
I grew immune to disappointment.

To trust someone who was once a stranger
Is like driving while blindfolded.
I had no clue where we would go.
I just prayed I didn't end up broken
If the infatuation got lost.

I wasn't sure if you were the one
Or just another one
That would push me away
Once we got too close.

As each day turned new,
I looked forward to learning
More about you, because you spoke
With so much truth.

My heart was drowned
By lies so many times.
But as soon as you arrived,
Your sincerity was a breath of fresh air.
You didn't chase your truth
With bourbon lies.
You gave it to me straight,
No rocks and I enjoyed every drop.

The Beauty Behind My Darkness
by
Michael Tavon

Enamored by your candor,
I became drunk off your words.
I knew if I touched your flames,
My palms would never feel a burn.

The Beauty Behind My Darkness
by
Michael Tavon

Epiphany

There was no denying it.
Your presence was effervescent,
Drawn by your mystery.
Our connection is magnetic.
As time progressed,
You became threaded
Into the fabric of my life.
I knew nothing would tatter us apart.
Allowing myself to open up again
Was the most beautiful epiphany
My heart has ever felt.

The Beauty Behind My Darkness
by
Michael Tavon

At first sight
Our chemistry
Became the perfect blend
Of everything right,
Our connection —
An undeniable science.

The Beauty Behind My Darkness
by
Michael Tavon

Love Prose

What I appreciate most about us is how
You and I are gifts to each other.
Our passions align.
Our auras vibrate on the same frequency.
From the beginning we never struggled to understand
The language our love speaks.
It's a spark that sends waves; an electric feel.

We celebrate each other's wins and keep the egos
radio silent;
We don't compete, we complete.
This brand of love is rare;
It feels like a fairy tale.
I'm aware what we share is special.
Life wouldn't make sense without you.
Your effort will be matched every waking day,
To ensure your worth won't get taken for granted.

The Beauty Behind My Darkness
by
Michael Tavon

Wellness

It takes great strength
To love someone
Who doubts themselves
Into an anxiety attack.

When the well
Of my self-worth ran dry,
You poured faith into my soul
Till it overflowed.

Thank you for
Being patient with my mind,
And kind to my heart.
Your support pulled me
From the deep abyss
Of feeling worthless.

The Beauty Behind My Darkness
by
Michael Tavon

You are My Big Break

Baby, mute those thoughts
Of not being enough
Before temporary doubts
Become permanent lies.
Believe me when I say
You are my big break,
We've been endgame
Since the day we met.
I'll reassure your worth,
Until you realize you are the prize.

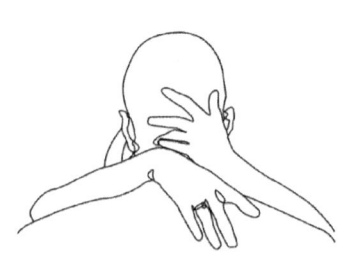

The Beauty Behind My Darkness
by
Michael Tavon

And I Appreciate That About You

You give me space,
When I need time
To myself but when
I pine for affection
You never starve me
Of your touch.

I get so sprung of
Every dose of your love.

You give me calm silence
And good conversation,
Tender loving and quality time.

You make me ponder
In a million ways I'm forever in debt
To your priceless advice,
My heart-shaped box.

The more I learn from you,
The wiser I grow.
Love is the greatest teacher
Of them all.

And some nights,
You humor me so wildly.
I choke on my own laughter.
You bring me to a different
Kind of climax, something
Impossible to name.

You've given my life balance.
You pour joy into
The cup of my hands.

The Beauty Behind My Darkness
by
Michael Tavon

Homesick Cure

As the sun said farewell,
Time and time again,
I felt more homesick,
For a place, I've never felt nor seen,
But I knew my heart belonged there.

I searched to and fro,
For this place, I missed but never visited.
When I wandered upon you,
My soul felt the heaven emitting
From your eyes.
I was smitten.
My homesickness was slowly cured
By the grace of your aura.

The Beauty Behind My Darkness
by
Michael Tavon

The Anticipation: The Arrival I

I knew it was real when you faced your fears
By boarding your first flight to see me.
You were a small-town girl following her heart.
I was the boy raised in the big city, searching for a fresh start.
It *sounds like a film for Hallmark.*
More things could've gone wrong than right, but you
Still took the chance.
You believed I was worth killing the distance for.
Before you, I grew accustomed to no one going the
Extra mile for me,
But you traveled one thousand three hundred and
eighty miles to be next to me.
We spent the weekend together.
Time passed like molasses was in our hourglass
Because the universe wanted every second to last.
You were brave enough to travel alone to see me,
The man you talked to (on the phone) for a few months.
I was determined to not let you down.
We had the vision to see what we could be,
And our dreams manifested into reality.
We both gambled with our hearts and hit the jackpot.

The Beauty Behind My Darkness
by
Michael Tavon

My hazy days became clear
Since you crossed my mind.
A pleasant surprise, I can finally
Rest my eyes.
You're the gateway to a blissful life.

The Beauty Behind My Darkness
by
Michael Tavon

The Anticipation, the Arrival Part II

"Wake up, we're here," you said.
When I opened my eyes,
A new reality was born.
I wasn't in Florida anymore.
Welcome to Connecticut
The sign read;
Anxiety felt like a dead weight
Sitting on my chest
As my heart raced like a horse,
On the track. I had my mind made up,
There was no going back,
But I was still afraid
To embark on the journey ahead.
I left everything I knew,
To discover something new.
"Welcome home," you said.
We stared into each other's listless eyes
And shared a euphoric kiss.
The autumn breeze was brisk.
I was relieved to breathe new air
Despite my doubts, I knew.
My greatest decision was leaving
My old house, to build a new home with you.

The Beauty Behind My Darkness
by
Michael Tavon

Our First Month Together

The 24-inch TV
Sat 3 feet away
From our queen-sized
Air mattress.
The carpet was dirty
And worn out

The children upstairs
 Were jumping like their floor
Was a trampoline and our roommates
Screaming and shouting.
Across the wall,
We had very little peace
And very little space.
Despite having next to nothing,
We would spend
Countless hours
Conversing in our dimly lit room.
Our sweet romance
Was slow dancing,
And creating a new
Love language only we could speak.
We were all we wanted.
We were all we needed.
We made the best
Out of a crummy living situation
Because as long as we had each other,
Nothing else mattered.

The Beauty Behind My Darkness
by
Michael Tavon

Tanka

You shake tight my skin
When I dip in your honey
Pool. A summer cool
swim, Till it's time for fresh air-
A sweet exhale of warm climax.

The Beauty Behind My Darkness
by
Michael Tavon

Sonku

Lie with me,
Leave nectar
On my lips,
After a kiss
As we rave
Wild hot flashes.

The Beauty Behind My Darkness
by
Michael Tavon

I Always Knew

The root of your heart
Was a route worth traveling to,
When you didn't force me to pay the toll
For what they did to you.

There are no dead ends,
Just clear paths.
Rearview heartbreaks
Never held us back.
We built a bridge for our future.
There's no reason to tread to the past.

The Beauty Behind My Darkness
by
Michael Tavon

Devotion

I will lead your hopeless heart to a higher place,
so you will never feel pain.
I will guide your mind 'til you learn your worth
again.
You won't have to acquiesce to
a life that doesn't spark a fire in your soul.
I vow to bestow the devotion your body deserves.
No more hurting; I promise to prove I am worthy.

The Beauty Behind My Darkness
by
Michael Tavon

Things That Make Sense

Autumn trees have pretty leaves.
Summer has rain; spring has allergies
And you have me.

Winter has snow, the sky is blue,
The moon belongs to the night
And I belong to you.

Florida has heat; ATL has wild streets.
Cali got earthquakes.
And you will always belong to me.

Despite the season,
No matter the weather
In this world, you and I belong together.

The Beauty Behind My Darkness
by
Michael Tavon

Hand Crafted Love
(Power of Doubt IV)

Now and then, I still believe
I don't deserve you.
It's not because I think I am a terrible person,
Undeserving of happiness
Nor that you're too good for me;
It's deeper than that.
Or isn't it?
Maybe it's so simple.
My mind can't grasp why.
Your love was handcrafted
By God and tailor-made for me;
You fit me so perfectly.
A reality that sends tremors vibrating
Through my heart.
What if, thread tears and colors fade
And the memories we have
Begin to wash away?
I don't want to think
About losing you
Because it's a thought
That doesn't make sense.
It's time for me to mute
The doubt screaming in my mind.
We deserve each other,
Today, tomorrow, and in any timeline.
I won't trick myself into believing otherwise.

The Beauty Behind My Darkness
by
Michael Tavon

In My Palms

I pull you into me,
 And gently place your cheek
In my palm.

We kiss like two souls.
Who has done this
Lifetimes ago

The Beauty Behind My Darkness
by
Michael Tavon

The Languages

What language
Does your body speak
When it calls for me?

Sing *"Je te veux"*
When you need a hand to hold
During winter's cold.
Whisper, *Tienimi vicino*
When your soul feels alone.

The language your body speaks
Is far from basic.
The sensation racing
Down your spine
 Has got your heart palpitating.
Slow down baby,
Maybe we're moving too fast.
There's no need to rush
But… ven aquí querida
I need to see you.

If you starve for affection,
I'm here to feed you.
I won't mislead you.
My white smile is not deceitful.
Believe in me, baby *Farti Mia.*
Please say, *Nakutaka pia*
Take my hand if you feel the same.

The Beauty Behind My Darkness
by
Michael Tavon

Call my name in any language
My heart will understand.

A touch like yours
Don't come around often.
The rare delicate love you behold
Deserves to be handled with care.
I vow to never break you.

The Beauty Behind My Darkness
by
Michael Tavon

Before I Fall in Love Again

Baby, before I fall in love
I've got some healing to do.
I'm not ready to peel back
These layers for someone new.
I'd rather recover from my hurt,
Than put secondhand stress on you.

Baby, be patient,
I swear you did nothing wrong.
My last heartbreak left burns
I couldn't rub Neosporin on.

After all that 'simpin'
I was left with a sickness.
I don't want to heal through you.
Let time be my prescription.

This may be hard to tell,
But I'm doing this for you as well.
An unburdened version of me
Won't drag you through hell.

It would be selfish to love you
While I'm freshly damaged.
The wounds are still sore
And can't manage with a bandage.

Let's enjoy the luxury
Of learning ngseach other.
As I heal from the bruises
Of being misused.
You deserve a version of me
That's free from the anxiety
Of emotional abuse and trust issues.

The Beauty Behind My Darkness
by
Michael Tavon

Shower Games

The water that feels like summer rain.
Warm steam shrouds the air,
Crystal droplets race down your spine.
I lather the parts your arms can't find,
I soap your skin, as you do mine
Until every inch is rid of sweat and stench.

Then we lock lips
 As if we're under the Eiffel
Romance in the shower,
Innocent wet dreams,
Under hot streams.

Such a sweet gesture,
 Is to clean each other,
As we wash our lovely sins away.

But baby,
Before we lose track of time,
Let's step out and get dry.
I'd cry if the utility bill
Gets sky-high.

The Beauty Behind My Darkness
by
Michael Tavon

Jupiter + Mars

I hope this isn't awkward
But you're my Halley's Comet.
A woman like you,
Only arrives once in a lifetime,
With a vibe that made my dreadful soul
Feel alive in one night.
My eyes fell into heaven
When they landed upon your skin.
I'm too afraid to fall in love again
But I'm willing to risk a gentle descent
If you'll fall for me, even as a friend.
As I stress by second-guessing,
I hope I get a second chance to
Make a first impression.
Let's manifest something special,
Rise to the next level.
This feeling isn't fleeting.
I feel it in my bones,
A galactic romance,
And two wild hearts, free to roam.
We could radiate like supernovas
Until we find our way back home.

The Beauty Behind My Darkness
by
Michael Tavon

My Latest, Greatest Inspiration

Believing in myself seemed
Like an impossible dream,
And daunting thoughts
Of being a loser haunted my mind.

I treated my self-worth like dirt
Until I convinced myself I was undeserving
Of the life I yearned for.

On those anxious nights,
You'd hold me tight,
Stared deep into my eyes
And reassured my soul
With powerful words
To lift my spirits back up.

Your unwavering belief motivated me
To break down the walls my mind built
To block from my goals.

Self-doubt was the beast
You helped me tame.
Without you, I wouldn't be
Where I am today.

The Beauty Behind My Darkness
by
Michael Tavon

Full Moon & Soul Food

Rub my eyes too good to be true.
Even my wildest dreams
Couldn't see someone like you,
So heavenly; out of the blue-
An angel in disguise,
With a heart so true.

There's no bad news or sad hues
With the aura of a full moon;
Baby, you're in a whole mood.
Like grandma's cooking,
Be my soul food,
Give me a spoon
So, I can devour you
In the best way.

Any day with you
Is my best day.
You feel better than payday.
I haven't cried on mayday.
Since the day you said, "Hey"
You look good to me,
Shawty swung my way.
What songs did you have
Playing on Myspace?

Now I'm just rambling.

The Beauty Behind My Darkness
by
Michael Tavon

You have that effect on me.
Effectively, you provide affection.
Never neglect me
Because I need you.
There's no need to lie.
Looking at you
Is like staring into heaven's eyes.

The Beauty Behind My Darkness
by
Michael Tavon

Orbit

I didn't fall in love with you because of how you
Made me feel,
It was how selfless you are with your heart.
Those who know you are blessed to be in your orbit
Because when you care, it's unconditional.
You offer compassion without a secret agenda.
Being around you feels like Christmas every day,
Because you spread joy in every room you enter.
It's easy to fall in love with someone based on how
They make you feel,
But I fell in love with you after seeing how softly
You treat others too.

The Beauty Behind My Darkness
by
Michael Tavon

Little Bubble/The Tea

We reside inside our own bubble
Of happiness,
Viewing the world
From the inside, looking outward.

We have no desire to indulge
In the drama
That seems to loom over
The people around us.

We protect our peaceful realm
By keeping to ourselves.

We sip our tea.
While casually enjoying the tea,
We hear and see.

It's like watching reality TV
In real-time.

The Beauty Behind My Darkness
by
Michael Tavon

Nesters

Oh how I adore holding you.
You were born to nest in my arms
Free as a bird but deserves a place
To call home; when your wings are sore
From soaring high for too long.

In my arms is where you belong
Your safeguard from harm,
And your refuge from dirty storms.
I'll hold you for as long as you need,
My arms will never grow fatigued.
I'm too strong to let you fall.

Rest your head here and listen to my heart speak.
I will squeeze tight & gently.
I will never let you go; hold on,
Don't release.
Wear my arms like armor
For the days you feel weak.

The Beauty Behind My Darkness
by
Michael Tavon

A Toast to Moonrise

My drowsy eyes felt the daze
Of the eternal night in my mind.
Life was the opposite of bright.

Then, you arrived and gave my heart
A new reason to beat—feel alive.
It didn't take a whole day for me
To recognize your light, my moonrise.

So profound, like a full blue moon
Amid a cloudless sky,
I would gaze at you, smile and say
"Everything will be all right."

You held me down like gravity,
Actually, I refused to float away.
You became a mainstay, the safe space
I ran to when the pain stung like a cavity
With no gravity in your soul.

It was easy for me
To put my trust in your hands.
You came with no ulterior motives
Or twisted plans.

Please understand you were the realness
My heart needed.
So, it could
Beat again.

Toast to you, my moonrise!
Thank you for coming into my life,
When I needed light the most.

The Beauty Behind My Darkness
by
Michael Tavon

I Want You to Want Me Too

Come here, my dear.
I want you like Marvin Gaye.
My heart is a safe space.
After a long day, let's find a place
To dance the night away.

Like it's just oui in pariiii
It's you I wanna marry.
Falling all over again
Can be scary.
The last dude
Broke you down, how dare he?
I know your past was no fairy tale.
I won't bail, my holy grail.
Give me a chance, I won't fail.

Because I want you,
Every syllable is a symbol
Of my naked truth.
There are no well-dressed lies.
I won't disguise how I feel inside.
If I felt otherwise,
I wouldn't waste your time.

I want you.
Do you feel me?
I hope you do, because you wanting me
The way I want you,
Would be a dream come true.

The Beauty Behind My Darkness
by
Michael Tavon

The Desire

You crave for me
The way I yearn for you,
An undeniable connection.
No mixed signals,
We speak with clear intention.

We know what we want
Neither of us has to chase
Or play mind games.
As youth wanes, each day
Is precious time we won't waste.

We value each other's space
With shameless infatuation.
Our bodies speak the same language.
We rarely have miscommunication.

We're never bashful
When it comes to showing gratitude
For the things we do.
I adore this marvelous life with you.

We are not weighed down
By confusion or doubt.
We speak from the heart
When we talk it out.

The Beauty Behind My Darkness
by
Michael Tavon

A life without you
Is a life I never
Want to go back to.

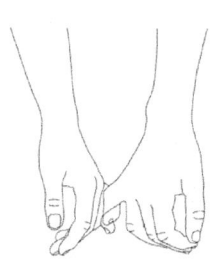

The Beauty Behind My Darkness
by
Michael Tavon

The Play Station

I would never play games;
I just wanna console you.
You're accustomed to being used.
Baby, I won't control you.

After a life of fear and despair,
Your heart will no longer
Endure wear and tear.
I promise to handle you with care.

The Beauty Behind My Darkness
by
Michael Tavon

Honestly

Before you arrived,
My life was a whirlwind
With little direction.

My mental health—neglected,
I was living recklessly.

Lackadaisical, lacking days of rest
Couldn't keep a job.
I didn't care how I dressed.

But you inspired me to believe
In my dream when I was on the brink
Of giving up.
You helped me see my worth
When you said, "You are enough."

I was incomplete without you.
You deserve every flower
I am about to give you,
Because your love is transformational.

The Beauty Behind My Darkness
by
Michael Tavon

I Need You/ You Complete Me

The way trees need leaves
And bodies need water,
I need your touch to help me feel stronger.

The way plants need sun,
The way oceans need air to flow,
I need your seeds of love to help me grow

The way cheetahs need speed
And giraffes need long necks to reach,
I need your gifts to make my life
A little bit easy.

I need you, I have no shame
In admitting it, I'm not codependent.
But in the most beautiful way you complete me.

You complete me.
Like a turtle without its shell,
I am naked without you.
Baby, can't you tell?

You complete me.
The way trees need rain,
You came and showered my pain away.

You complete me.
Like the four seasons of a year,
You made my worries disappear.

I need you; you complete me.

The Beauty Behind My Darkness
by
Michael Tavon

God is a Woman

She was everything my soul needed
When it felt depleted.

My heartbeat reached its crescendo
After years of feeling empty.
She restored the rhythm,
Her touch completes me.

She arrived and revived a dying hope.
If God is a woman
She is her.

The Beauty Behind My Darkness
by
Michael Tavon

The Blessing I Never Knew I Needed

Thank you for helping me forget
All the heartache I've endured.
I mean, the memories aren't completely lost
But since we found each other
The weight is easier to lift and
The pain is less prominent.

See, when I was alone,
I had more space
To dwell on each failed attempt.
At love, I was a perpetual loser,
Like the Chicago Bears.
It wasn't fair
How Cupid used me for
Target practice.

Because of you, I now view
Each heartbreak as a blessing
Because each one brought
Me closer to you.

The Beauty Behind My Darkness
by
Michael Tavon

Understanding

I never want to
End our day on a bad note.
Speak how you feel,
 And let it all go, the only way to heal through.
The problems we are facing
Is compassion and communication.

The Beauty Behind My Darkness
by
Michael Tavon

Alone Time and Quality Time

I love you.
I love being next to you.
I love having you under my arm during movie nights,
And during the long walks as we let the wind guide
Us to our destination, mini vacations to lively small
And towns.

I love dinners at home and small get-togethers with
family. I love trying new restaurants as we pretend to
be food critics. I love doing a million little things
with you, but I adore my alone, time too. My solitude
is where I find my space rejuvenated.

I would never push you away, or escape your
embrace, Sometimes, I need a little space
even if that means we sit in the same room without
filling the air with blank conversations.

Sometimes I enjoy feeling your energy without
activity. Sometimes I'd rather be in my own world
for a while before coming back to you.
I love everything about us.

When I require peace and quietude, you never pout
or make it about anything that it's not. You
understand me and encourage my urge for alone time.

You admire how I am wired.
Because after I recharge,
I am always down for some quality time.

The Beauty Behind My Darkness
by
Michael Tavon

Ivy II

My shaky heart slowed its pace
When you said you love me.
We fell so fast; we didn't see it coming.
No worries, the gentle rush
Didn't feel a hurry.

Even as an alien,
My heart recognized you
Like a UFO, it was rare finding you.

When you said you desired me,
I swear I heard you say
In another lifetime.
When I close my eyes,
I can see your smile.

When you said those words,
I was stuck in a trance,
A slow dance of emotions
Alone on our own floor.
You adored me, I adored you more.

The Beauty Behind My Darkness
by
Michael Tavon

Heat of War

In the heat of war,
I survive by the thought of you.
I refuse to leave this earth too soon.
Heaven can wait
Until I feel your lips again.

I rarely sleep but when I do,
My dreams are filled with you.
It's all I have to look forward to
When the sky is blue.

I promise to come back in one piece,
But more broken than before
When I come home.
Will you be there
To hold and console me?

After years of tears and fears,
I'm going to need you near.

I love you,
The iris of my eyes.
I refuse to die
Without you by my side.

The Beauty Behind My Darkness
by
Michael Tavon

Songs For Her Mood: Miguel's Groove

Like *candles in the sun*
My flame will never burn out
You're my *sure thing*
Whenever my mind gets clouded with doubt

You hit the spot like hot *coffee*
You got me higher than *pineapple skies*
Time flies like a *quickie*, skin covered in hickies

I'm falling like *leaves* in September,
Remember to *face the sun* when you look for me,

All I want is you; girls like you are rare to find,
Those feet must've jogged through my mind
For a thousand miles

Let my love *adorn* you *to the moon,*
My *Girl with the tattoo*
I get such a *thrill* when you
Come through and chill A feeling so real,

I feel anointed then you *arch & point*
what's the point in chasing
The fast life when the *simple things*
feels much better.

They say *what's the fun in forever*
But I've found the pleasure in knowing
You would never *use me*
In a bad way, let 'em tell it
This the life I wanna live
Til our *beautiful exit*

The Beauty Behind My Darkness
by
Michael Tavon

Your Person

Your person is somewhere
Praying that you don't give up
On the quest for true happiness.

They're building themselves up
From the essence of their flesh,
So, you feel the glow in their presence.

Thoughts of you
Float through their mind
Like a butterfly.
They're so eager to touch you
For the first time.

Your person sees you as the prize.

They will recognize
Your emotional scars
As beauty marks, the moment
You reveal the darkest pockets
Of your heart.

They will adorn you with
Their charm.
So don't give up
On the idea of togetherness.
Be ready when they come.

The Beauty Behind My Darkness
by
Michael Tavon

Reality, please
Don't pinch me
Any time soon.
It feels like a dream
When I sleep next to you.

The Beauty Behind My Darkness
by
Michael Tavon

I pine for you
When glimpses of your
Smile sprints through my mind.
I'm growing impatient
As I wrestle with time,
And eager to kill the distance
Between you and me.

The Beauty Behind My Darkness
by
Michael Tavon

Superman Without a Cape

I wanna fly to a perfect place
Where we can see eye-to-eye
And feel no pain.

I wanna penetrate your deepest
Mental state so I can elevate your brain
And make you climax from the soul.

My love is deep, my heart is gold.
Let's ride to never-never land
So we will never grow old.
 I know this world is cold and people
Are deceiving.
They make like the fall
When it's hard and start leavin'

Please believe me when I say,
My Lois Lane, I'm here to save the day.
No time to waste because I am already late.

How could I be fly without my suit or cape?
You take my breath away
When we lock lips like C.P.R.
You are my nova,
 A shooting star.

Just know I am always near,
No matter how far you are, my angel,
And I will be around
At every angle,
To protect you from pain, boo.

The Beauty Behind My Darkness
by
Michael Tavon

Fast Times At...

I no longer chase the high times
And fast life, as my young age begins
To chase nostalgic highs.
I want to see life through sober eyes,
And move at a softer...
Slower pace, before I fade.
The way today will become the past.
I yearn to feel the things I missed
When I was living life too fast.

The Beauty Behind My Darkness
by
Michael Tavon

Lifeline

In case you ever forget
How important you are to me,
Let this serve as a reminder.
You're the reason
Why my sun rises.
Without you, my life
Would be devoid of light.

The Beauty Behind My Darkness
by
Michael Tavon

Odyssey

After so much turmoil,
It was odd to see love
In its purest form
On this odyssey.
But honestly, I am thankful
I stumbled upon you
Without tripping.
Finding you made
This turbulent voyage
Called life worthwhile.

The Beauty Behind My Darkness
by
Michael Tavon

Baecation, Let's Go Somewhere

Let's have a brief break from the mundane.
Let's craft future nostalgia
Out of the moments.
We're afraid to say goodbye to
Let loose, break free,
And be as wild as we want to be.
We'll sip chilled champagne,
And skinny dip
In a wineglass Jacuzzi tub.
Get catered to like celebrities,
Our gratuity
Will make waiters
Brag to their colleagues.
 Let's spend daylight
Indulging in activities.
For so long,
Our mouths will grow sore
From smiling too much.
Love's most precious expression
Then, we'll rest
In a heart-shaped bed,
A short gateway from home
With my dearest one.
We work so hard;
We deserve rest.
That's the truth.
Let's explore the world
While we still hold our youth.

The Beauty Behind My Darkness
by
Michael Tavon

My pillow is laced
With thoughts of you.
So, when I sleep,
My dreams come true.

The Beauty Behind My Darkness
by
Michael Tavon

Tanka

Love is a gamble.
Would you push all your chips in
For a chance at bliss?
scared money don't make money,
Die alone or take the risk

The Beauty Behind My Darkness
by
Michael Tavon

Invented Love

I was told
Love is ugly and hellish
And if you manage to survive
You'll find your gold.
At the end of the cave
They said,
Pain is part of the game
And lovers are just enslaved.
By the rules,
We just play to lose
But not you.
As a rebel against the status quo,
You invented a new love,
The kind that doesn't
Require struggle.

The Beauty Behind My Darkness
by
Michael Tavon

Sweet Jazz

When your lips reach mine,
A taste of heaven
Dances on my tongue
Like sweet jazz.
You move me.
Joy fills my bones.
I'm yours,
And you are mine.
I've earned the right
To be proud.
When you kiss me,
I'm reminded of the
Heaven I have found.

The Beauty Behind My Darkness
by
Michael Tavon

Haiku

Let's make heaven wait,
Fructify Earth with more life
Till death do us part.

The Beauty Behind My Darkness
by
Michael Tavon

Things I Would Never Do

As the person who loves you,
Here are some things I would never do:

I would never depreciate your self-worth
Until you begin to question your work.
Baby, your priceless love is worth spending
My life with ten times over.
I will never take you for granted.

I would never allow jealousy to sit at our table,
As we feast on the fruits of our labor.
My hand will never swipe food off your plate.
I will always say grace and celebrate
Your success.

I would never cut my tongue
to keep a secret hostage,
My truth will be soft and unbothered.
Through my triumphs and struggles,
Honesty will be at the forefront.
You will never be left in the dark, I promise.

 I would never clip your wings.
Sky's the limit and beyond
For you. I believe in your potential.
You deserve to see it through.
No dream will seem delusional,
Because my faith will help you
Fly higher than you're used to.

I promise, each
Facet of your existence
Will be adorned and protected.
Your boundaries, I will respect.

The Beauty Behind My Darkness
by
Michael Tavon

I will never neglect the parts
Of you that needs to be watered.
From now to the moment,
You meet me at the altar,
I vow to be everything
Your heart, soul, and mind need,

The Beauty Behind My Darkness
by
Michael Tavon

Things I Will Always Do

As the person who blithely vows to spend
The rest of my days with you,
Here is a list of things I will always do:

I will always create placidity where turmoil enters.
I will hold your hand and guide you
Back to your center.

I will always make you laugh until
Your sides grow tired, simply 'cause
Your smile is my favorite site.
I will encourage you to be
Your greatest self,
Even when you don't believe
In your own strength and wealth.
My encouragement will
Nurse your self-esteem
Back to full health.

Pick our sheets over the streets.
Next to you is the only place I wanna sleep.
My untamed days are obsolete,
You will never feel the need to compete.
You are my big break;
You make my life complete.

I will make you see yourself
Through my eyes,
When those scars stop
You from seeing
How beautiful you are.

I will always say *I love you*

The Beauty Behind My Darkness
by
Michael Tavon

Like a mantra,
When in doubt.
Love is the answer
No cancer shall advance
In this universe of us.
Life is our stage
And we are two lighted-footed dancers.
(That was corny but I'm sure you got a kick of it)

I actually have one more thing to say:
I will always discover new ways
To sing your praise.
The joy you bring to my days
Is worth every ounce
I'm pouring into you
For every little thing you do,
I will reciprocate it back to you.

The Beauty Behind My Darkness
by
Michael Tavon

Triple Haiku

My love is a song,
A wild genre of its own.
It can't fit in a box.

Freestyle to my love,
Let the music carry you
Be who you are, free…

Please my easy friend,
Take off your cool, dance for me,
No rules for this tune.

The Beauty Behind My Darkness
by
Michael Tavon

Tanka

My pulse swings like jazz.
When you love me down at night,
Our bed is center stage.
Dance like no one is watching,
You are the star of this show.

The Beauty Behind My Darkness
by
Michael Tavon

Sonku

Be my peace
Like sunset views
On the beach.
Ease me sweet
Like tides on
Sanded feet.

The Beauty Behind My Darkness
by
Michael Tavon

Never Divided

I promise to be the opposite
Of closed off, and always open up.
Even with our clothes off,
The division between us will
Not exist.

The Beauty Behind My Darkness
by
Michael Tavon

Daydreams of a Lonely Boy

As I trotted to the central station
To avoid missing the bus,
I thought of you.

As the back of my neck cooked
Under the beaming sun
On my way to work,
I thought of you.

I spent half of my work day
Thinking about you
And none of it was a waste of time.

When I got home,
The anticipation of your voice
Sent electricity rushing
Through my tired bones.

Thinking of you
Made each day
Worth working through.

When I couldn't touch you,
The thought of you wasn't enough,
But I made due.

When I could no longer settle
for the thought of you,
That's when I knew
I was falling in love with you.

The Beauty Behind My Darkness
by Michael Tavon

Triple Haiku

When you call my name,
A sensation fills my bones.
Your voice is a rune.

Under your voodoo,
I'm fixed on you beyond words,
My name is water.

It flows off your tongue
With no strife, love is fluent.
Babe, my name is yours.

The Beauty Behind My Darkness
by
Michael Tavon

Sonku

Love is the
Tree that gives
Life to those
Who don't break
Branches or
Tear its leaves.

The Beauty Behind My Darkness
by
Michael Tavon

Spotlight for a Superstar

I am so proud to witness
Your growth from the front row.
I pat my hands together
To create the sound
Of a gentle thunder
As I marvel at the wonder
Of this transformation.
You deserve a standing ovation
But the show is far from over.
May I get an encore?
I am your number one fan.
Your spotlight will never
Get crowed by my ego.
The stage is all yours.
I love all that you are,
And everything you're becoming.

The Beauty Behind My Darkness
by
Michael Tavon

Pre-Wedding Day Jitters

A restless night haunts me,
The dark room crowed
By white noise.
Time ticks the way my heart beats—
Audacious and impatiently,
They both hate being told to wait.

I'm ready to fill this suit and tie
With my skin and bones
And marry my new home.

This is the first time
Anxiety has been good to me.
My tongue doesn't trip over my words.
Hives aren't scattered all over my skin.

My nerves are boiling.
 And my eyes stretched wide.
It's so hard to sleep
When the rest of my life
Is a mere 48 hours away.
I feel it in my palms,
Love is a special place to be.

The Beauty Behind My Darkness
by
Michael Tavon

The Night Before The Reception

She decorates the room with
Lights and new life.
I never thought anyone
Would be this thrilled
To become my wife.

I guess once upon a time
I convinced myself
I was nothing special,
But she proved me wrong.

She dresses the tables
With white sheets
And gold plates
And plans the seating chart,
While the rest of us
Cover the walls with
Vines and butterflies.
I smile as I watch her vision
Come to life.

My wife, my wife, my wife:
Those words taste so sweet.
I get a sugar rush thinking
About us.

She's my bride, my pride.
This woman is magic
And then some...

The Beauty Behind My Darkness
by
Michael Tavon

The Ceremony

As the heat of the day rises
And the sun rests on my skin,
Sweat gently descends
From my forehead into my eyes-
Both are surrounded by wetness
Like islands, I float down this aisle.
As if a nervous breakdown didn't
Overcome my body ten minutes prior;
But I'm stronger than I was before.
I stand proud in this suit,
I'm no knight in shining armor.
 I'm just a man eager to
Spend 100 years with you.
The groomsmen and
The bridesmaids take
Their places one by one
Until they clear the room for you,
Gliding down the aisle
With the man who raised you.
Stuck in a glimpse of time,
Breath stopped pumping
Through my lungs.
My eyelids put up a good fight.
They couldn't stop the tears
From falling into my wide smile,
With snot running down my nose
You've never been more beautiful.
You stare at me, with those eyes
I've fallen for a thousand times,
But this one hits different.
I can't really explain it,
This moment stands before us.
I was only anxious

The Beauty Behind My Darkness
by
Michael Tavon

Because I was ready
To say I do.
All the stress leading up to this day
Is irrelevant.
I am finally at the altar
With your hands in mine.

The Beauty Behind My Darkness
by
Michael Tavon

Shifted Forever

My entire world shifted
When you put that ring
On my finger,
No longer bare, as a gentle air
Waved through my tiny hairs.
Now I wear a symbol of your vows,
A small gesture of protection
From my misguided youth.
I stand in a new beautiful truth.
This ring is my daily reminder
That I deserve a lifetime of happiness.
When we sealed the deal with a kiss,
My entire world shifted on its axis,
My finger turned to gold-
A symbol I will proudly wear
Till I am one hundred years old.

The Beauty Behind My Darkness
by
Michael Tavon

I'm So Happy to be in Love With You

All the little things you do,
Like when you come home from the store,
With a small gift or two, just to say
These things reminded me of you
Or the way you look at me,
When I bite into the food you cook for me
To see the expression of my face,
Each taste always feels like a warm embrace, your passion to fulfill me
Can't not be replaced

Each day I fall for you more and more
My heart was made just for you,
That's why love never worked
with anyone else before
Affection galore, the way you touch
tickles my skin. Gentle like a feather
Driving like a feather in the wind,
You're my one true friend

I'm so lucky, I never have to
Search for love again

I'm content and in bliss,
The way we kiss like it's the first time
Or when you console me when I cry
I never have to hide who I am how I feel
I often rub my eyes to ensure this love is real
You are living proof that dreams do come true
And I am so happy to be in love with you

Printed in Great Britain
by Amazon